Annette Feldman's
Needlework
for the Home

Annette Feldman's
Needlework for the Home

Photography by Doug Long

A RUTLEDGE BOOK

Prentice-Hall, Inc., Englewood Cliffs, N.J.

ACKNOWLEDGMENTS

It is to those companies listed below that the author wishes to extend a special word of thanks for their having, throughout the years, endeavored to supply the best of materials to foster the joy of handcrafting in our country; and a very special thanks for their total cooperation in supplying beautiful materials toward the making of the various projects in this book.

Emile Bernat & Sons Co., Uxbridge, Massachusetts
Coats & Clark, Inc., Stamford, Connecticut
Columbia-Minerva Corporation, New York, New York
Reynolds Yarns, Inc., New York, New York
Spinnerin Yarn Co., Inc., New York, New York
William Unger & Co., Inc., New York, New York

Thanks to Mr. and Mrs. Fred R. Sammis, Mr. and Mrs. Allan Mogel, Mr. and Mrs. Thomas Knudsen, and Dr. and Mrs. Michael Gindi for the use of their homes in the photographing of the following craft projects.

Photography Stylist: Susan Morrow
Line Artist: Liney Li

Prepared and produced by Rutledge Books, Inc.
Distributed by: Prentice-Hall, Inc., Englewood Cliffs, New Jersey.
First Edition 1978
Printed in the United States of America

Library of Congress Cataloging in Publication Data

Feldman, Annette.
    Annette Feldman's Needlework for the home.

    "A Rutledge book."
    1. Needlework. I. Title. II. Title: Needle-
work for the home.
TT751.F44   746.4   78-10690
ISBN 0-13-036897-0

CONTENTS

Dedicated
In Loving Memory of My Parents,
Gertrude and Emanuel Gerber,
and to
My Husband, Irving,
and
the loyal and faithful members of my
staff—Marjorie Williams, Antonia
Builes, Valerie Kurita, Bertha
Zeltser, and Julie Burgess—to all
of whom I am grateful for having made
the production of this book possible

INTRODUCTION

Although very few of us group around the piano in the parlor these days to hum the melody and sing the refrains of the early nineteenth-century best-seller "Home Sweet Home," all of us do know, without perhaps even being aware of their origin, those famous words that say "Be it ever so humble, there's no place like home." Home is that wonderful place that, once we have entered and closed the door behind us, belongs to us alone and to those, whether family or friends, with whom we share our living quarters. It is our own private world where, away from the outside one, we can kick off our shoes, let down our hair, and even stand on our head or walk on our hands if that's what we really want to do. More than this, it is within the confines of the home that our real life takes place. We live and love there, we laugh and cry and hope and pray there, and when we want to, we open our door for friends and welcome them to our own inner sanctum.

Some of our homes are green, some are blue, and for those of us who like pink, our quarters might be a combination of pink and olive, or pink and orange or brown. Whatever color it is and whatever style we have chosen to live in—whether it be period, contemporary, or as eclectic as we want to make it—it is ours, the most perfect reflection of our total personality and a place of which we are proud, especially today. For a period of years, there was a restlessness among many of us, a time when the house seemed to be the place we wanted to run away from. Perhaps it was the tension of the war years that caused this, or perhaps it was just the result of a number of societal revolutions that were taking place then. Whatever the reason, however, the age of running seems to have passed, and most of us look forward now to spending a large part of our leisure time at home, relaxing from what might have been an otherwise either very exciting or too routinely dull day, usually occupied with work or with one of the many different types of activity we are involved with these days. Once more we enjoy entertaining at home, or being entertained in someone else's home, or just quietly relaxing by ourselves or with our family.

It is with this new life-style in mind that we have written this book for you. Statistically, there are nowhere in the entire world two homes that are exactly the same. To enrich the one you live in, and make it even more individually your own, we have created and are presenting now within the covers of this book a large group of exciting and beautifully handcrafted designs that can be made for every part of your house. There are here unusual wall hangings and floor coverings, and charming and sometimes whimsical small and large decorative accessories, fun things for kitchens and bathrooms, and a very delightful group of things for outdoor use in the garden or patio. The variety of crafts involved runs a complete gamut, including knitting for those who relax most to the steady, rhythmic clicking of a pair of needles in their hands, and crocheting for those who enjoy this craft most; hairpin-lace work; and latchet hooking for others who like to work with a hook, a piece of rug canvas, and some yarn, perhaps even having the work spread out on a large table where friends can work along with them, all hands working together to create an unusual rug or wall hanging. Beyond this, there are things to make with embroidery and needlepoint, and others involving painting, macraméing, weaving, and working with paper, pasta, and dried beans and flowers. Clear, easy-to-follow instructions are included right along with the presentation of each project; in addition, sections have been included offering stitch explanations and guidance toward the perfection of all craft work.

Many of the designs are presented in such a way that you can adapt them to fit your special size needs as well as change the colors to suit your color scheme. Our grospointed area rug, for example, was made with fifteen squares to measure a total of twenty-seven by forty-five inches, and it was embroidered with vividly colored flowers on a natural background. The instructions for this rug tell how you can easily, by making more or fewer squares, adjust the size to make anywhere from a twenty-seven- by thirty-six-inch rectangle to a nine- by twelve-foot room-size rug. Of course, if you choose to change the size and perhaps use pastel flowers on a black background instead of our vivid colors on a natural one, you will have succeeded in creating a totally individual floor covering that suits your needs and that is different from any other floor covering anywhere.

Because being your own designer in this way is such a pleasurable experience, we have, in creating the exciting ideas in this book, allowed you freedom to work them out to your own satisfaction. You could weave shutter inserts for your windows with ribbon and parcel twine instead of rickrack and heavy rug yarn, as we did ours, or be innovative with the number of bottles and selection of plants you want to use for the rooting plant arrangement for the kitchen wall, as well as varying the sizes and shapes of the bottles. Your choice of a dried flower arrangement on the hairpin-lace wall hanging stretched over mirror glass would certainly be a very personal thing, as would the size and shape of the pasta with which you want to define the design on your "beaded" macramé curtains and the color you want to paint the individual pieces of pasta.

In short, there is fun galore in this book—craft fun to make your own "house beautiful" more beautiful, to occupy your leisure hours, and to encourage your participation in some form of gratifying creativity. Indeed, it would be our pleasure to know that these were but a few of the joys you will have gained by looking through the pages of this book and deciding to work out at least one, hopefully several, of the interesting projects appearing on those pages.

Some Guide Rules for the Perfection of Your Handwork

On the pages of this book are many very interesting projects to be made for the home—for your home, and for whatever reason they might appeal to you. While some have been designed for fun and others to enable you to create something that will fulfill a particular need in your living environment, almost everything appearing here wants to say something to someone who loves "home," who enjoys handcrafts, and who would like to make something personal which, when done, will be something very special, after having already satisfyingly filled many hours of "doing" toward this end. Many of the projects involved are very contemporary, and several others have a traditional flavor; most, however, are comletely unique. If you like them as we hope you will, they should make you happy in whatever setting you live. A variety of crafts is involved, too. Some of the things to make are knitted and some crocheted; others are made of hairpin lace and macramé; there are also those that involve working with pasta and seeds and paper and paints, with latchet hooking and various forms of embroidery. In this chapter now, to help you create a more perfect piece of craft work, something beautifully handmade rather than "homemade with tender loving care," we offer important information for the preparation of, the actual working of, and, very important, the final finishing of whatever it is you have decided to make.

Much of the work involves little more attention than that you would be giving to anything you are doing that you want to be done right—a little forethought and a careful logistic planning as to what material and equipment you will need to make your effort worthwhile. All your materials should be on hand before you start to work, and they should be durable and of good enough quality to warrant the work you will be doing with them. When you are using yarn or fabric, you need to be especially careful that you have bought enough to complete your project, thus not running the risk of having to change dye lots when you are halfway done.

Very important in your work, too, is the attitude with which you approach it. If it is to be a work of pleasure, then let it be so. Begin your project with a feeling of confidence that you are going to make something really beautiful, which, when done, will satisfy you for a very long time to come. Tension or nervousness does, unfortunately, reflect itself in handwork, whereas an easy approach helps to give it the smooth, finished look you want. Be assured that by carefully reading the written instructions, once overall to get the feeling of what you will be involved with, and then following them step by step as you go, you cannot help but create a fine piece of work.

Most of the projects in this book are actually quite simple—neatness and the taking of accurate measurements are really the only prerequisites for making them. Pasta and paper and seedcraft fall into this category, as does the art of painting, too. Macramé, the simple practice of knotting originated by early seamen who found the making of knots an interesting way of filling long, empty hours while at sea, can be done well with the use of good materials, an even tension, and a careful step-by-step following of instructions. For latchet-hook work, the other knotting art, the stitches are outlined and your tension already gauged for you by the openings on the background canvas on which the work is done. The art of making a piece of hairpin lace is again quite a simple one, requiring only careful attention to the instructions for the project being made and an observance of the basic guide rules given above—the purchase of a sufficient amount of good materials, a relaxed, even tension on your part, and a neat and careful finishing.

There are a few needlework skills, however, for which special guide rules do apply. Knitting and crochet work and needlepoint and embroidery are perhaps just a little more involved, and you should be aware of other basic principles important to doing this kind of work correctly. Toward this end, we offer the following information to help you create beautiful handwork in these areas too. We also offer advice on a few finishing techniques that apply to most of the crafts, a knowledge of which will help you to put the final touch to your completed project.

For Knitting and Crochet Work

Gauge: Gauge is an all-important, magic word, the degree of observance to which can spell the success or failure of your knitting and crochet work. It means the "tension," or number of stitches and rows you are working to an inch. The instructions for each project in this book involved with either of these two crafts are accompanied by a specified gauge. To achieve the perfect size of whatever you are making, you must see that your gauge is exactly the same as that called for. To be sure that your work will measure correctly, it is always necessary that you make a 3- or 4-inch-square swatch with the yarn, needles, and stitch you are going to use and then measure your swatch on a firm metal ruler or stitch gauge. If you are getting more than the prescribed number of stitches per inch, try larger needles or a larger hook; if you are getting fewer, make another sample piece using smaller needles or a smaller hook. The little extra time you devote to testing your tension before starting your actual piece of work will be very well worth the effort made.

Joining yarn: When you join a new ball of yarn, always do it at the beginning or end of a row, even though the old ball of yarn may run out in the middle of a row and a small length of yarn may need to be wasted. In both knitting and crocheting, the new yarn is attached at the end of the last row that was finished with the old yarn and the next row is started with the new yarn.

Changing colors: When a change of color in knitting is being made at the start of a new row, simply work the last stitch on the last row with the old color and start the next row with the new. When it occurs, however, somewhere along the row, always bring the new color to be used from under and around the color just dropped so that the yarn is twisted and the work lies smooth and flat. When working in this way, the color not being used must always be carried loosely across the back so that it does not pucker the stitches being worked. In crocheting, when there is a change of color somewhere along the row, the last stitch of the original color is worked with that color until just two loops of that last stitch remain on the hook. Those two loops are then removed with the new color. When the change occurs at the start of a new row, the last two loops of the last stitch on the row just finished are the ones that are removed with the new color.

Ripping: Sometimes while knitting or crocheting, you will discover an error several rows after it has occurred. Your choice is either to rip it out or to overlook it and probably always be aware of it, even though the error may involve only one stitch. Surely, it is best to take your first medicine and rip. If the error is just a dropped stitch in a knitted piece, you can pick it up relatively easily with a crochet hook. To do this, insert the hook into the dropped stitch, *catch the loose strand of yarn on the next row in back of the hook, and pull the loop through on the hook. Repeat from the *, working up each row until the top strand has been pulled through. Then place the last loop on the left needle and continue with your knitting. If the mistake is more major, however, and ripping is necessary, withdraw the needles from your work, rip to one row below the row in which the error occurred, and then rip out the next row, stitch by stitch, inserting one of the two free needles into each stitch as you go. When all the stitches have been picked up in this way, you can continue with your knitting again. In crochet work, ripping is an equally painful although much simpler procedure. Since each row and each stitch is complete in itself, there is no need to pick up stitches after having ripped back to where the error has occurred. In this case, rip to one stitch before the error, insert your hook into that stitch, and continue with your crocheting again.

For Embroidery Work

Background fabric, needles, and thread: Both for the ease of working and the general appearance of your finished piece, it is important that you choose the proper background fabric for your embroidery work. An even, open-weave fabric on which the space produced by the angle of the vertical and horizontal threads is visible is the best type to use, since the threads can be easily counted and, consequently, a greater degree of regularity can be achieved in the actual stitching. Linen is very often the best choice because its surface is hard enough not to pull or pucker while being worked on and its weight is usually heavy enough to accommodate the weight of the embroidery threads being drawn through. Monk's cloth and burlap are also good choices for a heavier type of embroidery. The cut size of whatever material you use should be at least 1 inch larger on all four sides than the actual piece of finished work, and the four sides should be bound with masking tape before the work is started in order to prevent any fraying of the edges. Needles should be sharp-ended and of medium length for ease of work; they should also have long, slender eyes suitable for threading multiple strands of yarn or thread but shaped so that they will not form a hole in the material when being drawn through. When several colors of thread are being used, it is wise to work with more than one needle to avoid the abrasive wear and tear caused by frequent rethreading.

Enlarging a design: To enlarge a design for embroidery, trace the design and then transfer it to graph paper, using a sheet of carbon between. Box in the design on the graph paper so that you can count how many squares have been used; then draw a box on another piece of paper to the size you wish the finished design to be. Divide this into the same number of squares as the first one, and copy the design, square by square, onto it. To copy a curved line across several squares, mark where it crosses the squares and then join the marks.

Transferring a design: The transferring of a design onto material is a relatively simple procedure, although it should be done very carefully since a little patience at this time will ensure a smoother and more accurate design to work with. To make the transfer, place dressmaker's tracing paper, carbon side down, on the right side of the fabric and lay the traced design on top. Then trace over the design with a pencil, being careful to hold the design securely in place so that the tracing does not become distorted yet holding it lightly enough so that the carbon won't smudge the material.

For Needlepoint

Stitching techniques: You are ready to start stitching once you have cut and taped your canvas in the same manner as described for the preparation of the background material for embroidery work. For ease in working, cut the yarn to be used to a comfortable length, usually about 18 inches. Thread your needle so that the short end of the yarn does not extend more than 2 or 3 inches beyond the needle eye, since the constant drawing of double yarn through the canvas will cause an uneven tension in your work. When starting with a new strand of yarn, do not knot the end; instead, leave a 2- or 3-inch strand free on the wrong side of the work. Work the first four or five stitches over the free strand on the back and then cut off the remainder. When coming to the end of a piece of yarn, draw your needle through to the underside of the work, turn the canvas over, and, working on the wrong side, weave your needle over and under every other stitch just completed for about 1 inch; then cut off the remaining end of yarn. To further ensure a more perfect piece of work, avoid possible distortion by working different areas of the canvas rather than proceeding directly from one corner or edge to the opposite one. Also, although a single thrust of the needle from top surface to top surface may be a faster and easier way of working, thrusting it up and down with two separate motions will help to relieve the pull on the mesh of the canvas.

Blocking: Usually it is necessary to ease a finished piece of needlepoint back into shape by blocking it, since some amount of distortion does occur during the working process. An easy and good way of blocking is to pin your piece right side up on a board, being sure to use rustproof pins or tacks and to have the corners at perfect right angles and the parallel sides stretched to exactly the right length. Dampen the canvas and leave it pinned until it is completely dry; then press it lightly if desired.

General Finishing Techniques

Seaming is often necessary as part of the finishing process. There are three popular methods of seaming:They can be either woven, sewn, or crocheted. In all three instances, it is important to have the pieces to be joined carefully matched. In those cases where yarn is involved, use the same yarn as that with which the pieces were worked. *Woven seams* are worked with a blunt-ended tapestry needle on the right side of the finished pieces. The needle is inserted through the first stitch on one edge, drawn through two strands along the edge, and then worked through two strands on the opposite side edge. *A sewn seam* is also worked with a blunt-ended tapestry needle and with an approximately ¼-inch-long running backstitch or an overcast stitch on the wrong side of the work. *The crocheted seam* is worked with a fine crochet hook on the wrong side of the work (sometimes on the right side for design effect when so specified in instructions) with either a single crochet or a slip stitch worked through the thicknesses of the stitches on each side of each of the edges to be joined. For sewing projects, seaming may be done either by machine or with the use of the running or overcast stitches.

Blocking or pressing, the final finish to any piece of work, is also necessary in almost all needlecraft and sewing projects. This may be done either before or after the pieces are assembled. Where needlecraft and yarn projects are involved, unless otherwise instructed, lay the work flat, cover it with a damp cloth, and press it lightly with an iron, allowing steam to form and keeping the iron moving over the piece. Most pieces made with synthetic yarns will have little resiliency to them, so that they will remain close to the size to which they were made; wool pieces, however, and even some cotton can be stretched slightly, if desired, while the piece or pieces are still damp. For projects made of fabric, it is important to follow the "care" rules for whatever fabric you are using.

ABBREVIATIONS

beg	beginning	p	purl
ch	chain	pt	point
CC	contrast color	rep	repeat
dec	decrease	rnd	round
dc	double crochet	sc	single crochet
dp	double point	sk	skip
dbl tr	double treble	sl	slip
hdc	half double crochet	sl st	slip stitch
inc	increase	sp(s)	space(s)
k	knit	st(s)	stitch(es)
lp(s)	loop(s)	tog	together
MC	main color	tr c	treble crochet
psso	pass slip stitch over	yo	yarn over
pat	pattern		

WALL HANGINGS

A Contemporary Wall Hanging

Measuring a big 2½ by 3 feet, this unusual, very bold wall hanging is made with some colored paper, a small amount of lightweight cardboard, and a few skeins of yarn. It is very bright and contemporary in design, and its importance on a wall in any modern setting belies the little effort and small cost involved in the making of it.

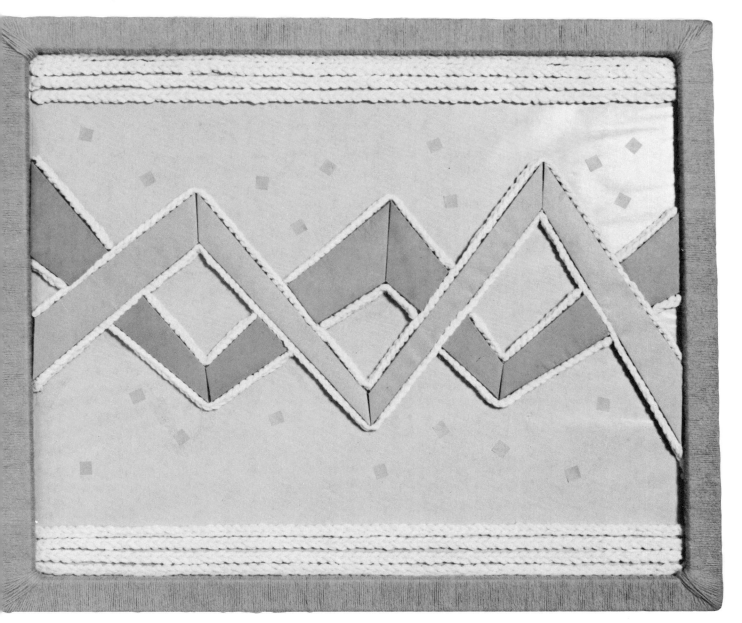

Materials:

1 sheet glossy gift-wrap paper, 30 × 36 inches, in hot pink
1 piece heavyweight cardboard, 30 × 36 inches
rubber cement
1 piece lightweight cardboard, approximately 18 inches square
3 sheets art paper in medium blue and 3 sheets in coffee, each 12 × 18 inches
2 skeins (4 ounces each) Columbia-Minerva knitting worsted, in colonial blue
canvas stretcher
white glue
wood staple gun
aluminum crochet hook, size K
4 skeins (2 ounces each) Columbia-Minerva Nantuk Bulky, in winter white
2 screw eyes and a length of fine wire (for hanging)

The Hanging

With rubber cement, adhere the pink paper to the heavy cardboard. Then cut twelve pieces of the lightweight cardboard, enlarging and following the patterns in illustrations A-1 and A-2. Using the same illustrations, cut four pieces

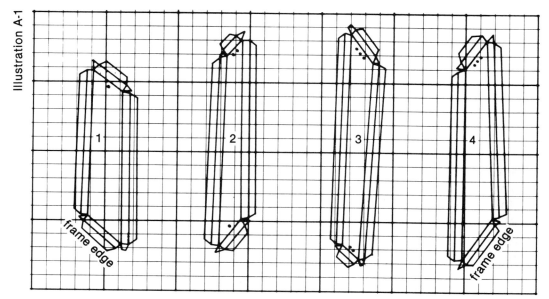

Each square = 1 square inch

Fold under on each line of each piece. Outer tab is to be folded under and glued to background. Small tabs should be tucked under and secured to adjacent side piece.

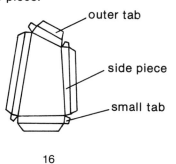

outer tab

side piece

small tab

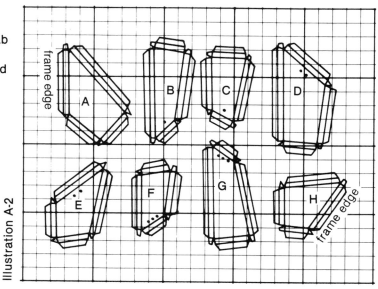

16

of the blue paper and eight pieces of the coffee. Cement the colored papers onto the cardboard pattern pieces and, following illustration B, arrange and ce-

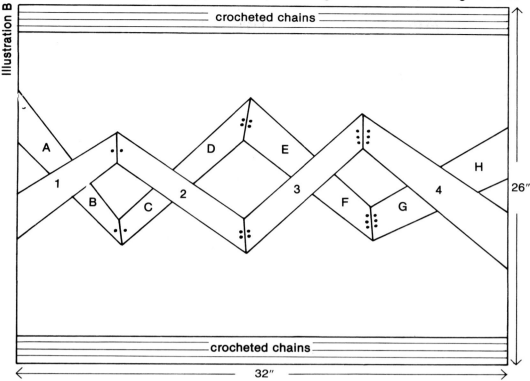

crocheted chains

A

D E

H

1

2 3 4

B C

F G

26″

crocheted chains

32″

For placement of pieces, match dots and follow the above chart

ment them to the background, wedging them into place and leaving 2 inches uncovered all around. Now join the four parts of the canvas stretcher for the frame and cover it with the blue knitting worsted yarn, carefully winding the yarn around and around it, keeping the strands close together so that no parts of the wood are exposed. Wind several times around the corners to make sure that these parts are also completely covered. Secure the end of the yarn at the start of the winding process with a little white glue; also use it to secure any other loose ends.

Finishing: Staple the partially "painted" heavy cardboard under the covered frame. With double strands of the bulky white yarn, crochet two chains, one long enough to fit around the entire top edge of the now-joined blue pattern pieces and the other to fit around the entire bottom edge of that strip. With the white glue, adhere the crocheted chains in place, positioning them flat along the edges to be covered. Then crochet ten chains of different lengths to fit around the component parts of the coffee-colored pieces and glue them in place. Again with double strands of the bulky yarn, crochet eight more chains, each approximately 30 inches long. Fit four of these along each long edge of the composition, placing the two outer ones at the top and bottom close to the frame and each of the remaining set of three spaced approximately ¼ inch apart. Adhere these in place with the white glue. Finally, cut nineteen ¾-inch squares of blue paper and glue them to the composition either at random or as shown. Finally, insert the screw eyes and attach the wire so that the finished piece will hang either horizontally or vertically, as desired.

One Hanging Planter to Hold Several Plants

Hang this handsome macraméd planter in any room in the house, fill it with lush green ivy and philodendrons, and add a stunning focal point to that area. Or hang it from a patio awning and set it with dripping fuschia plants. Worked in tiers, the planter is 7 feet long and designed to "house" several plants. A variation of just a few simple knots makes for its beautiful texture, and the addition of two brass rings, a round tray measuring 16 inches in diameter, and large unraveled-yarn tassels adds to the overall effect.

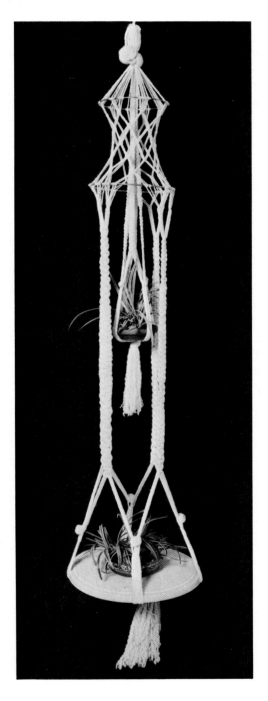

Materials:
6 skeins (4 ounces each) Bernat Berella Bulky, in natural
rubber bands
2 metal rings, one 8 inches in diameter and the other 10 inches, in gold
round tray, 16 inches in diameter

The Planter

Cut eight strands of yarn, each 40 feet long, for the short inner planter and six-teen strands, each 56 feet long, for the outer planter. Fold all the strands in half and tie them together in the center with a single strand of yarn measuring ap-proximately 36 inches. Suspend all the hanging strands from a ceiling hook, us-ing the 36-inch strand as the hanging loop. Leave this strand fully extended when you start your work and then draw it shorter, pulley-fashion, as you move on down toward the bottom, in this way always allowing yourself a comfortable working position. Now tie a slipknot 7 inches below the top center fold, using all forty-eight hanging strands to tie the knot. Separate the sixteen short strands from the thirty-two long ones, placing sixteen of the longer strands on either side of the short strands, which are now in the center and ready to be worked on. To prevent the many cords from becoming tangled, roll each of the long strands into a small ball and secure it with a rubber band. Then, working with the short strands only, divide them into four groups of four strands each and make a 33-inch-long sinnet (a series of tied knots forming a vertical column) of square knots on each group. Continuing to work with these strands only, take two from one group and two from the adjacent group. Leaving 4½ inches of these four strands unworked, make a square-knot button, finishing off the bot-tom of the button with the second half of the square knot. When this first button has been completed, make three more in the same manner with the remaining strands, tying them at the same level of the work. Now leave 8 inches of the strands unworked, and finish the inner planter with a large slipknot, using all sixteen strands. Finally, trim the remaining hanging strands to an even 9 inches and unravel the end of each one to separate the three plies of the yarn and give it a curly look.

Now work with the thirty-two long strands for the outer planter. Leaving 6½ in-ches of each of these unworked, measuring from just below the large slipknot at the top, fasten each one separately to the 8-inch metal ring, spacing them evenly around the ring and tying them on with a horizontal double half-hitch knot. Leave 1½ inches unworked. Then make eight square knots all at the same level, using four of the thirty-two strands for each of the knots. *Again leave 1½ inches unworked and then make eight more square knots, this time with two free strands from any knot made above and two from the adjacent knot above. Repeat from * three times. Now leave 1½ inches unworked and make another group of horizontal double half-hitch knots like those around the 8-inch ring, this time spacing them evenly around the 10-inch ring. Leave 1½ inches unworked and then make eight square knots, using two adjacent strands from each of the groups of knots just above those tied onto the 10-inch ring. Leave 3½ inches unworked now, and working with eight strands, make four square-knot sinnets, each measuring 26 inches. Start the first group of knots with four strands each from two adjacent groups of knots on the row above, and use the center four strands for the filler and the outer four strands for the working cords. Finally, leave 6 inches unworked, make four 8-strand square-knot buttons with four strands from the end of one sinnet and four from the end of an adjacent one, leave 13 inches unworked, and then make a large slipknot with all thirty-two strands. Trim the remaining hanging cords to an even 12 inches and then unravel the ends as for the inner planter. Insert the tray into the now-finished outer planter, just above the large slipknot at the bottom.

A Hairpin-Lace Wall Hanging Trimmed with Dried Flowers

This unusual and charming conversation piece is surprisingly easy to make and one much to be admired. Shaped to an octagon, straight strips of natural-colored mercerized-cotton hairpin lace form an elegant note when stretched over 12-inch mirror tiles and adorned with stalks of dried wheat and a few sprigs of natural dried flowers.

Materials:

adjustable hairpin-lace loom
aluminum crochet hook, size C
2 balls (175 yards each) Coats & Clark's "Knit-Cro-Sheen," in color #103
needle and thread, in natural
4 self-adhesive mirror tiles, each 12 inches square
1 piece plywood, 3/8 inch thick, 24 inches square
household cement
masking tape
1 spray can shellac
assorted dried flowers, including one circular, flat piece approximately 3
    inches in diameter, and wheat stalks
2 screw eyes and a length of fine wire (for hanging)

The Hanging

First strip: With the loom adjusted to 3 inches, work 64 lps on each side of the loom. For the inner edge, sl st 4 sts tog 16 times and join the end of the strip with a sl st in the first st to form a circle. Fasten off. Sew the spine ends together. For the outer edge, *sc 2 lps tog, ch 5, rep from * around, and join the rnd with a sl st in the first sc. Next rnd: Work 1 sc in each sc and 4 sc in each ch-5 sp around. Join this rnd with 1 sc in the first sc and fasten off.

Second strip: Adjust the loom to 3½ inches and work 128 lps on each side. To finish the inner edge, sc 2 lps tog, *ch 2, sc 2 lps tog, rep from * across, ch 1, and turn. Next row: *1 sc in next sc, 2 sc in the next ch-2 sp, sk 1 sc, 2 sc in the next ch-2 sp, rep from * across. Join the last sc with a sl st to the first sc to form a circle. Fasten off. Sew the spine ends together. Pin the inner edge of the second circle to the outer edge of the first circle and sew these two edges together with an overcast stitch. For the outer edge, *sc 2 lps tog, ch 5, rep from * around, and join the end of the rnd with a sl st in the first sc. Next rnd: Ch 1, sc in the joining, work 1 sc in each sc and 4 sc in each ch-5 sp around. Join the rnd with a sl st in the first sc and fasten off.

Third strip: Adjust the loom to 4 inches and work 256 lps on each side. Finish both the inner and outer edges of this strip in exactly the same manner as the inner and outer edges of the second strip. Then pin the inner edge of this circle to the outer edge of the second circle and sew these two edges together.

Finishing: Adhere the mirror tiles to the plywood to form a 24-inch square. Center the hairpin-lace piece on the mirror and cement its center to the mirror center. Now gently stretch the hairpin lace toward the bottom edge of the mirror, stretching it until it measures about 10 inches from the center—6 inches of the mirror should remain uncovered on either side. Cement this edge in place and hold it with tape until the cement has set. Then remove the tape and repeat the same process on the remaining three sides of the piece. When all pieces have been cemented in this way, an octagonal shape of lace will have been formed on the mirror. To complete the composition, apply a triple coat of shellac to the dried flowers and wheat to preserve them permanently, allowing drying time after each coat. Cement the single flower over the center of the hairpin lace. Then form a spray of wheat stalks and other long, slender flowers and place it so that it extends from the center of the piece toward the top right- or left-hand corner. Finally, trim each of the four corners with an arrangement of small dried flowers. To hang the composition, twist the two screw eyes in place on the back of the plywood and thread them with wire.

Kumquat, the Cat

Kumquat, who sits in a field of wheat under a pretty blue sky, can be an always-there friend for any child, needing little more care than some occasional talk-to-each-other companionship. Kumquat is made of a furry white mohair yarn fringed onto an open-mesh knitted background; his features are formed by reembroidering the background, his eyes are oval glass beads, and the wheat is made of a few balls of polished wrapping twine. Creating Kumquat is easy fun and you will be making a best friend for some little child you know and love.

Materials:
1 skein (4 ounces) Spinnerin Marvel Twist Deluxe Knitting Worsted,
    in sky blue (A)
1 pair straight knitting needles, #5
tapestry needle, #18
3 balls (1 ounce each) Spinnerin Frostlon Petite, in natural (B)
small amount Spinnerin Marvel Twist Deluxe Knitting Worsted,
    in dark brown (C)
5 balls (100 feet each) polished wrapping twine (D)
needle and thread, in natural
aluminum crochet hook, size C
2 oval-shaped glass beads, each 1 inch in diameter at widest point, in brown
white glue
approximately 8 inches ribbon or braid, 1 inch wide, multicolored
small amount stuffing material
wooden frame with cardboard backing, 1¾ inches wide with an outside
    measurement of 22 × 30 inches, in natural

Pattern Stitch: *Row 1*: K 2, *yo, k 2 tog, rep from * across the row, and end with k 1. *Row 2*: P. Repeat Rows 1 and 2 for the pattern stitch.

Gauge in Pattern Stitch: 5 stitches = 1 inch

The Hanging

With A, cast on 79 sts. Work even in pat st until piece measures 25 inches (this measurement allows for stretch after the fringing) and then bind off. Block the piece into a rectangular shape. Complete the color-A portion of the work by embroidering, with double strands of yarn and the tapestry needle, a cross-stitch over the background area of the picture indicated on the chart, using each hole of the knitted stitches as the stitch through which to work the embroidery. Then fill in all areas of Kumquat with fringing, following the chart for color. Cut strands for the long color-B fringe to 4 inches, for the short color-B and C fringe to 2½ inches, and for the D fringe to 7 inches. Count each hole in the knitted stitches as the stich through which to to be short to approximately ¾ of an inch; the long, color-B fringe to approximately 1½ inches; and the longer, color-D fringe to approximately 3 inches. Tack all the D strands in place with needle and thread after they have been drawn through the knitted holes so that the twine doesn't slip out of place. Reembroider the face markings and legs now as indicated on the chart, using the C yarn and tapestry needle. Then glue on the eyes and the ribbon for a collar, and randomly glue bits of stuffing material to the untrimmed background to make clouds. Finally, frame the piece, allowing the long, color-D fringe to hang over the frame for a three-dimensional effect.

□ within cat outline = short fringe in B
□ outside cat outline = short fringe in A
× = long fringe in B
/ = short fringe in C
• = long fringe in D

Line markings for face and legs
are worked in an embroidered
outline stitch with double
strands of C.

A Seashell Composition

A collection of shells picked from along a sandy shore can be easily transformed into the dramatic contemporary wall hanging shown here. Very few additional materials besides the shells are needed to complete this composition, the assembling is an easy job, and since seashells are always one-of-a-kind, your piece will be completely unique.

Materials:
1 picture frame, ¾ inch wide, 10 × 13 inches
approximately 3 quarts seashells, in assorted sizes, shapes, and colors
household cement
a string of simulated pearls, in any size
1 piece plywood, 1 inch thick, 6 × 9 inches
1 spray can (32 ounces) metallic paint, in silver
½ yard metallic fabric, 36 inches wide, in silver
1 piece plywood, 3/8 inch thick, 16 × 20 inches
masking tape or wood staple gun
1 skein (1 ounce) Columbia-Minerva Camelot Metallic Yarn, in silver
aluminum crochet hook, size F
1 picture frame, 1½ inches wide, 18 × 22 inches
4 nails, each 1½ inches long
1 piece brown wrapping paper or lightweight cardboard, 18 × 22 inches
2 screw eyes and a length of fine wire (for hanging)

The Composition

Remove the glass from the smaller picture frame and put it aside for another use. On the cardboard backing provided with the frame, cement most of your collection of shells in whatever arrangement pleases you, superimposing shell upon shell to form your own design and adhering each shell firmly and carefully. Next, cement a number of single pearls to the composition, placing them at random. Now, center the piece on the 6- by 9-inch piece of plywood and firmly cement it in place. Spray the entire piece, including the outer edges of the plywood, with silver paint. Cut the metallic cloth to measure approximately 18 by 22 inches. Stretch it over the 16- by 20-inch piece of plywood and wrap the excess fabric over the edges to the back. Tape or staple the fabric edges in place. Now crochet the piece of silver mesh to be stretched over the metallic cloth on the plywood. Working to a gauge of 5 chains to 1 inch, ch 141. Sk 9 ch, sl st in the tenth ch, *ch 11, sk 9 ch, sl st in the next ch, rep from * across the row and end with a sl st in the last ch, ch 11, and turn. Next row: *Sl st in the sixth ch of the next ch-11, ch 11, rep from * across the row and end with a sl st in the last ch-11, ch 11, and turn. Repeat the last row until the piece measures approximately 16 by 18 inches, unstretched. Fasten off.

Finishing: Stretch the crocheted metallic mesh over the metallic cloth and tape or staple it to the back of the plywood. Remove the glass from the 18- by 22-inch frame, glue the remaining shells and pearls at random to this frame, and spray it with silver paint. Set the large piece of plywood into the underside of the frame and cement it in place. Then hammer the four nails in place to hold the small piece of plywood to the larger board, hammering one nail through the outer plywood into each of the four corners of the inner one. Finally, back the composition with wrapping paper or lightweight cardboard. Attach screw eyes and wire for hanging the finished piece.

A Primitive Head
"Painted" with Dried Beans

Truly a work of art, this unusual wall hanging is easily made with little more than a small amount of natural seeds and beans, a cut of linen cloth, a skein of embroidery floss, and a piece of thin plywood.

Materials:

1 sheet paper, at least 16 × 18 inches, in white
dressmaker's tracing paper
1 piece natural linen, 19 × 24 inches
1 skein 6-strand embroidery floss, in brown
crewel needle, #4
embroidery hoop, 6 3/8 inches in diameter
1 piece plywood, ¼ inch thick, 17 × 22 inches
masking tape or wood staple gun
approximately ½ pound each of medium-sized red kidney beans (A),
    green split peas (B), barley (C), small white beans (D),
    and small black turtle beans (E)
white glue

The Head

On the sheet of paper, enlarge the design to 16 by 18 inches. Then, with the dressmaker's tracing paper, transfer the design to the linen, centering the design on the cloth. Embroider the piece as indicated. Center the finished piece on the plywood, fold the remainder of the cloth to the back of the board, and secure it in place with masking tape or staples. Finally, following the chart,

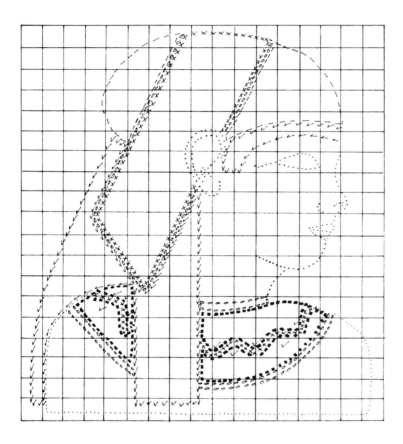

Each square = 1 inch

Key for Embroidery and Placement of Beans
All dotted lines to be embroidered, using the outline stitch
Large areas outlined with X's to be filled in with A
Large areas outlined with O's to be filled in with B
Large areas outlined with □'s to be filled in with C
Large areas outlined with — to be filled in with D
Large areas outlined with ↙ to be filled in with E
Single lines or individual symbols to be filled in according to the symbols above

glue the beans to the design, arranging them in the directions shown in the photograph. The most efficient way to adhere the beans is to dot glue over a 2-inch-square area of the portion to be covered and then lay the indicated beans on the glue; repeat this process to completion.

FLOOR COVERINGS

A Hairpin-Lace Area Rug

On a bare floor or over existing carpeting, this beautifully designed area rug could well become one of the focal points of your home. It is 36 inches wide and 44 inches long, not including the unusual braid, fringe, and tassel trim along each short edge, and it's made of a soft, machine-washable-and-dryable bulky yarn in a natural color.

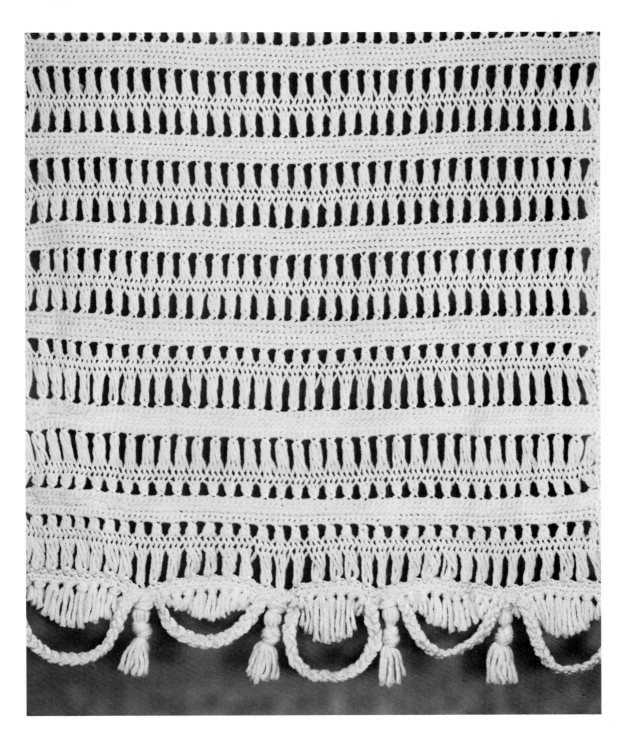

Materials:
6 balls (4 ounces each) Bernat Berella Bulky, in natural
adjustable hairpin-lace loom
aluminum crochet hook, size K
tapestry needle, #18

Gauge in Single Crochet: 3 stitches = 1 inch

The Rug

With the loom adjusted to 4 inches, make nine strips of hairpin lace, each with 108 lps, three of them with the spine in the center and six with the spine 1 inch in from one outer edge. Finish each side of each strip in the following way: Attach yarn to the top of the strip, *sc 3 lps tog, ch 2, rep from * across the strip, and end by working 3 lps tog, ch 1, and turn. Next row: Work 1 sc in each sc and 2 sc in each ch-2 sp across, ch 1, and turn. Next row: Work 1 sc in each sc and fasten off. Arrange the strips according to the chart and sew them together with an overcast stitch. Then work 2 rows of sc along each long edge of the rug, working 1 sc in each sc across the row and 2 rows sc across each short edge, as follows: Row 1: Work 1 sc in each row of the sc edging of each strip and in each spine end and as many sc in each of the end long and short lps as are necessary to make the work lie flat. Then ch 1 and turn at the end of the row. Row 2: Work 1 sc in each sc across. Fasten off.

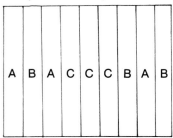

Arrangement of
Hairpin-Lace Strips

| A | B | A | C | C | C | B | A | B |

A = Short loops to be placed to right side of strip
B = Short loops to be placed to left side of strip
C = Strips with center spines

Trim

Braided loops: Crochet six chains, three for each edge of the rug to be trimmed (the short edges), making each chain approximately 6½ yards long. Then braid three of the chains to make a strip measuring 70 inches, knot the end, and cut away any excess yarn. Now divide and mark one short edge into fifths. Arrange the braided strip along the edge as shown in the photograph, making a loop between each marker. The loops at each end and the center should measure about 12 inches; the lps on either side of the center lp should measure about 10 inches. Tack the braid in place at each marker. Braid the remaining three chains and with them trim the other short edge of the rug in the same manner.

Tassels (Make eight): Cut eight strands of yarn, each 14 inches long. Holding the strands together, fold them in half and knot the pieces together with a length of yarn tied approximately 4 inches down from the fold. Using four tassels for each short edge of the rug, knot one onto the last sc row between each of the braided loops. Trim the ends of each tassel to measure 2 inches below the large center knot.

Fringe: Cut a number of strands of yarn, half of them 6 inches long and half 8 inches. Using double strands, knot nine of the 6-inch strands into the last sc row above each of the 10-inch braided loops and nine of the 8-inch ones above each of the 12-inch loops. Finally, trim the ends of the fringe to follow the contour of the braided loop below each set of fringe, allowing 1½ inches between the ends of the fringe and the top edge of the braid.

A Rainbow Afghan, p. 86; Irish Knit Pillows, p. 88; A Grospointed Area Rug, p. 45.

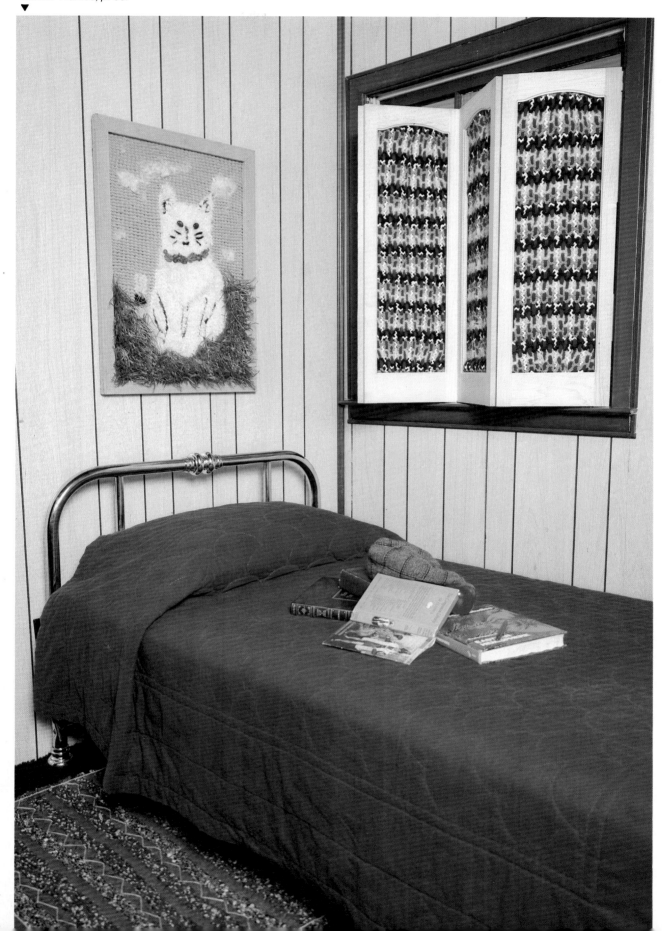

The Braided Rag Rug

Two and a half yards each of three different colors of fabric, each 45 inches wide, were used to make this cozy braided rug. It measures 24 inches wide by 36 inches long, has reembroidered cotton trim, is very durable, and is also very easy to make. Although we bought new fabric for our rug, you can, if you choose, use whatever remnants of fabric you might have in your own scrap bag, cutting them into strips and then piecing together as many of them as you need to reach the proper braiding length.

◄ "Stencilled" Fabric for a Child's Room, p. 52; Percival, A Life-Size Life-Time Friend, p. 66.

Materials:
2½ yards cotton fabric, 45 inches wide, in brown (A), 2½ yards in a small all-
    over print (B), and 2½ yards in another small allover print
blunt-ended needle and carpet thread, in brown
1 ball (100 yards) Coats & Clark's "Speed-Cro-Sheen," in natural
aluminum crochet hook, size D

The Rug

Cut twenty-seven 1½-inch-wide strips of color A, thirty of B, and thirty of C, each the full length of the material. Fold under, to the wrong side, approximately ¼ inch along each long edge of each strip and press these folds in place. Now, with A, make the first braid in the following way: Holding the ends even, tack three strips together approximately 2½ inches in from the end. Make the first twist of the braid, hang the loop just made over a hook or hanger for a comfortable working position, and then braid the entire length of the strip to within 2½ inches of the bottom. Tack these ends in place as you did the top. In this same manner, make eight more color-A braids, ten B, and ten C.

Finishing: Arrange the twenty-nine braided strips in the following order: one A, three B, one A, three C, one A, two B, one A, two C, one A, two C, one A, two B, one A, three C, one A, three B, and one A. Weave the strips together as they are arranged, using the carpet thread and following the illustration for the weaving process. Then approximately 2 inches in from each short edge, stitch securely across the braids. Finally, remove the original tacking threads and trim the extended strips, beyond the sewn line, to an even length. For the cotton thread trim, mark out four zigzag lines, placing these markers along the length of the second and fourth color-A braids in from each long edge and evenly spacing the markers 2 inches apart. Now, with triple strands of "Speed-Cro-Sheen," work out the pattern, laying the thread flat and tacking each turn of the zigzag with the same thread and an overcast stitch. To complete the rug, crochet a chain with double strands of "Speed-Cro-Sheen" long enough to fit around the four edges of the rug. Sew it in place, again with the same thread, placing it over the stitched line at each short edge and just inside the first and last color-A braid along each long edge.

Knitted Numbered Stair Treads

Our knitted stair treads, which were made to cover the steps and seat of one of the popular, standard kitchen stepstools, display bright red numbers knitted into a white stockinette-stitch background. To emphasize the numbers, one tomato has been worked into the lower step, two into the other step, and three into the seat, almost giving the effect of the illustrations in a child's learn-to-count book. Covered with clear plastic, the treads are practical, too, for they can be easily wiped off with a damp cloth when they become soiled.

Complete instructions are given for making the step covers that appear here, although they can be adjusted to cover any size and type of step, as we explain below. We have also included charts for the numbers and tomatoes, as well as one for the alphabet. The full number chart will guide you toward the marking of any number of stairs you choose to cover, and the alphabet chart that appears along with it will help you to spell out any whimsical message you may want to add or substitute, whether it's just the simple words *up* and *down,*

or maybe *play* for steps leading to the playroom, or *Andy* if he is the one occupying the bunk at the top of a ladder, the steps of which you want to cover. If your steps are larger than ours, you can easily enlarge our numbers and letters by extending them widthwise for as many boxes as desired, counting one box for each stitch to be covered, and then extending them lengthwise by the same number of boxes. This method of enlarging applies to the letters too. If you wish to use other decorative material, the simplest way to do this is to trace the design you've chosen over carbon onto graph paper and then, box by box, work the design into your knitted piece.

Since the steps we covered have a "lip," we knitted a ribbed border to cover that lip; the ones you make, however, may need to cover just a straight portion of a regular step on an average flight of stairs of any height. To cover these, simply cut a paper pattern to the size of the tread you want, decide on the number of stitches you need to work with by multiplying the size of the tread by the gauge of your knitting, and then work to that size, fitting in whatever designs you have chosen. In designing treads of this type, you might want to cover them with plastic and edge them with metal stripping or you might make them of a completely machine-washable yarn and then line the undersides with a nonskid latex material, again machine-washable.

Materials:
2 skeins (4 ounces each) Spinnerin Marvel Twist Deluxe Knitting Worsted in
     white (MC), 2 skeins in bright red (CC), and a small amount in bright green
1 pair straight knitting needles, #8
tapestry needle, #18
needle and thread, in white
aluminum crochet hook, size K
½ yard medium-weight clear plastic, 36 inches wide
1 yard narrow elastic, in white

Gauge in Stockinette Stitch: 9 stitches = 2 inches
                                  6 rows = 1 inch
Gauge in Ribbing Stitch: 4 stitches = 1 inch
                            6 rows = 1 inch

The Treads

First step: With MC, cast on 38 sts. Working in stockinette stitch throughout (k 1 row, p 1 row), work 2 rows even. Then inc 1 st at beg and end of every other row until there are 44 sts. Work even on 44 sts for 4 rows. Then, following the chart, start the pattern for the first step and work it for the 8 rows to completion. K 6 more rows even. Then dec 1 st at beg and end of every other row until 38 sts remain. Work 1 row even on these sts and then bind off. With double strands of CC, embroider an outline stitch around the number and the tomato. Then using the bright green yarn and the outline stitch again, embroider a 5-st stem at the top of the tomato, as shown in the photograph. To make the ribbed lip for the step, work as follows: For the back portion, cast on 32 sts with MC and work in k 1, p 1 ribbing for 2 inches; then bind off in ribbing. For the front and side portions, cast on 70 sts and then work in k 1, p 1 ribbing for 2 inches;

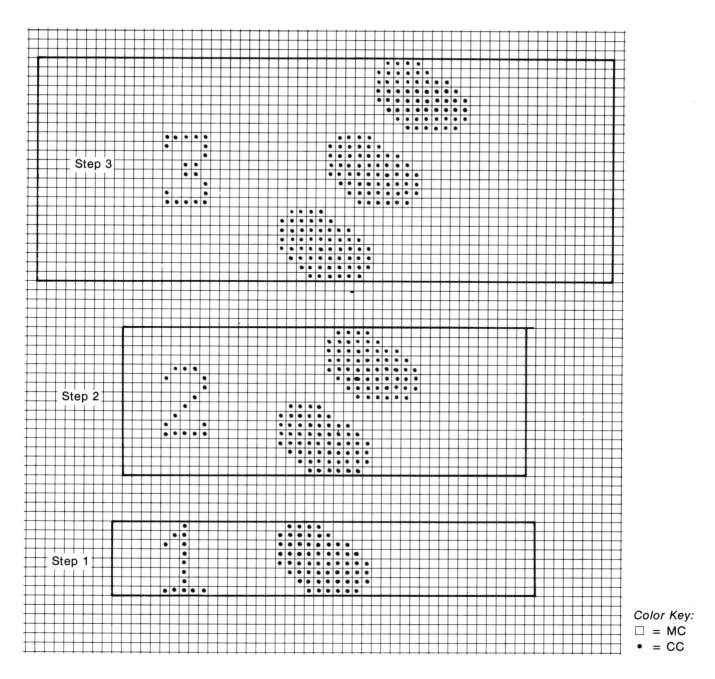

Step 3

Step 2

Step 1

Color Key:
□ = MC
• = CC

bind off. Sew the ribbings in place, attaching the back ribbing along the bound-off edge of the knitted piece and the other piece of ribbing along the other three sides. Now cut a piece of the plastic to the shape of the stockinette-stitch portion of the knitting and sew it in place along the seam line that divides that portion from the ribbed edging. Finally, with double strands of CC, crochet two chains, one long enough to span the bottom edge of the back ribbing plus 22 inches additional for tying and a second one to span the bottom of the ribbing that fits around the front and two sides, with 18 inches additional for tying. Make one more chain in the same manner to fit evenly around the edge of the finished top of the step. Sew the top chain in place over the joining seams of the edge of the plastic and the ribbed borders; sew the other chains to the bot-

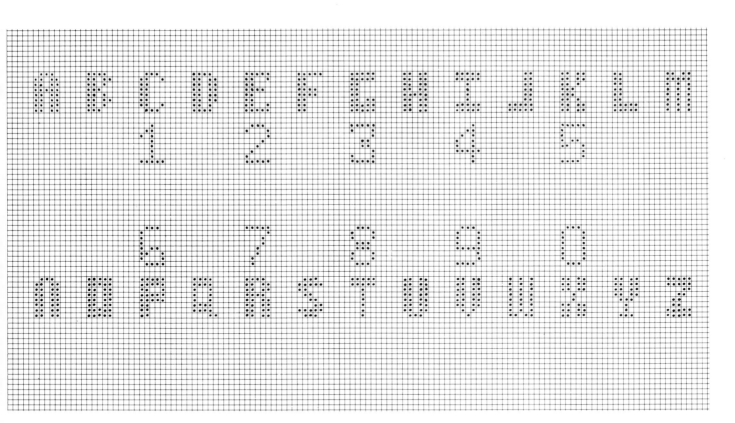

tom edge of the lip, leaving an equal amount of the extra chain extending at each end on these chains to allow for tying around the legs of the ladder.

Second step: With MC, cast on 36 sts and, again working in the stockinette stitch throughout, work even for 2 rows. Then inc 1 st at beg and end of every other row until there are 42 sts. Work even for 3 rows. Now start the pattern for the second step and work it to completion. When this has been done, work even in MC only for 3 rows. Then dec 1 st at beg and end of every other row until 36 sts remain, p 1 row, and bind off. Embroider around the numbers and the tomatoes as on the first step, and finish the piece as for the first step.

Seat: With MC, cast on 50 sts. Work even in stockinette stitch for 2 rows. Then inc 1 st at beg and end of every other row until there are 60 sts, work even for 5 rows, start the pattern for the seat, and work it to completion. Work now in MC only for 6 rows even. Then dec 1 st at beg and end of every other row until 50 sts remain. P 1 row and bind off. To finish this piece, embroider over the pattern as for the first two treads. To make the ribbed lip for it, work as follows: Cast on 150 sts to fit around the entire outer edge of the piece and work even in k 1, p 1 ribbing for 2 inches. Bind off. Cover the top stockinette-stitch portion with plastic cut to fit, and finally sew the ribbing to the bottom edge of the top portion. With double strands of CC, crochet two chains, each with a sufficient number of sts to fit around the top and the bottom edges of the ribbing. Attach the top chain for this tread as the other top chains were attached. Then cut a piece of elastic to fit around the bottom portion and sew the bottom chain over the elastic to hold it in place.

A Crocheted Contemporary Area Rug

Fifteen acrylic single-crochet squares join to shape this stunning 32- by 48-inch contemporary area rug, further embellished with an edging and an interesting 7-inch-long knotted fringe at both short edges of the piece. Each individual part of this "put-together" rug measures approximately 9 inches square; whatever size rug you choose to make will differ from ours only in the number of 9-inch squares you make. Do bear in mind, though, that when changing the size, the few rows of finishing around the outer edges and the fringe will add a little extra width and length to your piece.

Materials:
21 skeins (70 yards each) Columbia-Minerva Great Ideas, in russet
aluminum crochet hook, size K
tapestry needle, #18
needle and thread, in russet

Gauge in Single Crochet: 7 stitches = 3 inches

The Rug

Squares (Make fifteen): For each square, ch 21 and work even in sc on 20 sts for 25 rows. Then work 1 row of sl st and fasten off. Separate the squares now into two groups, eight marked A and seven B. Finish each group as follows: With double strands of yarn and working horizontally across the 20 sts, finish each of the eight A squares with ten superimposed rows of sc, making each of these rows by inserting the hook under each st, drawing the yarn through to the right side, and then completing the sc st on the right side of the work. Crochet these superimposed rows along the rows indicated on Chart A. In the same manner, crochet superimposed rows on top of the seven B squares, this time working only 4 rows on each square along the rows indicated on Chart B. Arrange the squares now in checkerboard style, following Chart C, and sew them together with an overcast stitch. Then work 4 rows of sc along each long edge of the rug and 2 rows along each short edge.

Finishing: With triple strands of yarn, make four crocheted chains of 70 sts each or long enough to fit across the width of the rug. Use these to cover the four joining seams as follows: Sew the end of one chain at the beginning of one seam. Then, following the seam line, draw it through the superimposed chains that form the design of the rug, drawing it through the center chain of the groups of three and the two center chains of the groups of four. Finally, sew the other end of the chain to the other end of the seam. Repeat this procedure with the remaining chains.

Fringe: Cut several pieces of the yarn into 15-inch-long strands, and knot nine of them in every other stitch along each short edge of the rug. Then, following the same pattern from each outer edge of each of these ends toward the center, wrap several strands of yarn around the first group of fringe 1 inch below the top knot, *the second group at that point and once again 1 inch below the first tied point, the third in both of those places and once more 1 inch below the second tied point, the fourth as the second, and the fifth as the first. Rep from * once and then tie the tenth as the second, the eleventh as the third, and the twelfth as the second. Knot the next seven groups of fringe as the first. Now, repeat the knotting process, reversing the order and using the twelfth knot just made as the first knot of this group. You should have thirty-one knots on each edge of the rug when you are finished. Trim the fringe ends evenly. Finally, with needle and thread or yarn, draw together, on the underside, the center of each of the three and four groups of superimposed sc chains, pulling the finishing threads tightly so that the straight sc cords pull in at the center of each of these groups and then billow out on either side.

Chart A

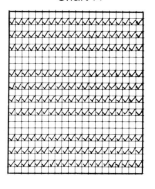

Chart B

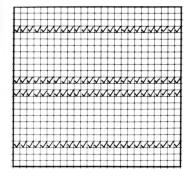

Chart C

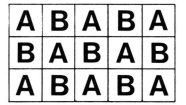

44

A Grospointed Area Rug

Made of fifteen 9-inch squares, some worked in solid color and others in a floral pattern, the rug shown here is designed in a checkerboard pattern and measures approximately 27 by 45 inches, without fringe. Since the piece is a composition of many small squares, the one you might choose to make can be of any size, either smaller than ours or practically room size, the only requisite being that it be a multiple of 9 inches in both width and length. You can vary the design as well, using more or fewer floral squares and arranging them in any pattern you like—perhaps one with an inside or outside border, a large flowered center, or in a solid color with a patterned arrangement in just one corner.

Materials:

1 piece rug canvas, 4 spaces to 1 inch, 30 × 48 inches
masking tape
blunt-ended embroidery needle
7 skeins (4 ounces each) Bernat Berella Bulky in natural (MC) and 1 skein each in new gold, orange heather, honey, scarlet, copper, frosty lime, and hunter green
1 yard lining material, 48 inches wide

The Rug

Cut fifteen pieces of rug canvas, each 40 spaces square, and then bind all the edges with masking tape. Embroider seven of the squares in MC only, using the Kalem stitch and filling in just the center 36 spaces on each square. On the remaining eight squares of rug canvas, embroider four following Chart A and three following Chart B, using the continental stitch.

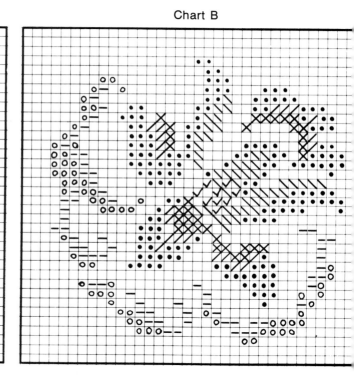

Chart A   Chart B

Color Key:
• = new gold
\ = orange heather
× = honey
/ = copper
↙ = scarlet
— = frosty lime
o = hunter green
□ = natural

Finishing: Turn the two unworked rows along each edge of each square to the underside and hem them in place. Arrange the fifteen squares checkerboard-fashion or as you wish, and then join them with MC and an overcast stitch. With double strands of MC, embroider both vertical and horizontal lines of cross-stitch over all the seam lines.

Fringe: Cut MC into 7-inch strands and knot two strands in every other stitch around the four sides of the rug, knotting the strands through the last rows of the embroidery. Trim the fringe ends evenly. Finally, cut the lining material to the size of the rug within the fringed area, adding ¼ inch for a turn-under, and sew it in place.

Pennsylvania Dutch Motif Doormats

Latchet-hooked and semicircular in shape, these mats have a traditional "hearts and flower" design and can be used either together as a 36-inch-in-diameter round mat for the inside or outside of the door or, for an interesting effect, one inside and one outside, the straight edges toward the riser.

Materials:

2 pieces rug canvas, 7 spaces to 2 inches, each 59 spaces long × 109 spaces wide

masking tape

12 skeins (2 ounces each) Reynolds Bulky Reynelle in cranberry (MC), 6 skeins in off-white (A), 3 skeins in turquoise (B), 1 skein in royal (C), and 1 skein in kelly (D)

latchet hook

needle and thread, in red

4 yards iron-on rug binding, 1½ inches wide

The Mats

Make two: Bind the edges of the canvas with masking tape. Cut a number of strands of the various colored yarns, each 4 inches long, and then, following the chart, latch 1 st in every space on every row to completion. When this part

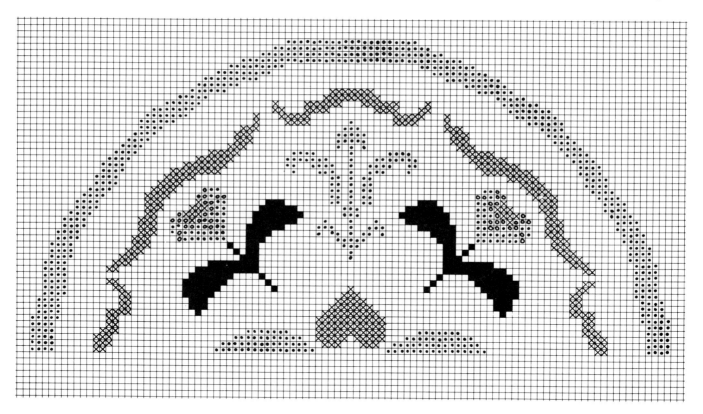

Color Key:
□ = MC
× = A
• = B
○ = C
■ = D

of the work has been done, cut the canvas to the shape of the finished piece but allow 4 unworked spaces around all sides. Turn these spaces to the wrong side of the work, hem them in place, and then complete the underside of the piece by covering the turned-under hem with rug binding. If the mats are to be used as one round piece instead of two semicircular ones, sew them together along the two straight edges.

WINDOW TREATMENTS

Grospointed Panel Trim and Tiebacks
for Your Own Draperies

A charming all over pattern is used for the trim shown here, designed to create a new look for your preexisting draperies and to add the always-admired touch of handwork to them. Although our side-panel trim was made for 8-foot-long draperies and our tiebacks are 60 inches long, the size of both can be easily changed to meet your own requirements. The small all over repeat of the pattern readily lends itself to such adjustment, which is accomplished by working either fewer or more repeats, depending on whether you need smaller or larger pieces. Since the yarn used is a bulky one and the canvas a large 4-space-to-1-inch one, you'll have no trouble making as large a piece as you wish in very little time.

Materials:

2 strips rug canvas, 4 spaces to 1 inch, each 5 inches wide (for the panel trim)
and 2 strips, each 7 inches wide (for the tiebacks) (*Note:* Length of each
strip should correspond to the length and width of your draperies)

masking tape

6 skeins (2 ounces each) Reynolds Bulky Reynelle in cranberry (A), 6 skeins in
natural (B), 2 skeins in kelly (C), 2 skeins in turquoise (D), and
2 skeins in royal (E)

tapestry needle, #18

needle and thread, in color to match your draperies

enough lining material to cover the backs of the rug, canvas strips

6 hooks and eyes

Color Key:
□ = A
/ = B
X = C
• = D
✓ = E

The Trim

To make the grospointed strips, bind the edges of each strip with masking tape.
Then with the continental stitch, embroider them, following the charts. Finish
the strips by cutting away any excess canvas, allowing enough excess to make
a 2-space hem along each edge. Sew these hems, line the pieces, and sew the
panel strips to the right side of the inner edges of the draperies. Finally, sew
three hooks and eyes along the short edges of each tieback to hold them in
place once the pieces have been drawn around the center of the hangings.

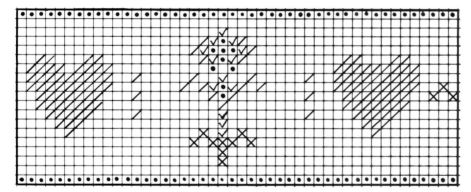

Grospointed Tiebacks

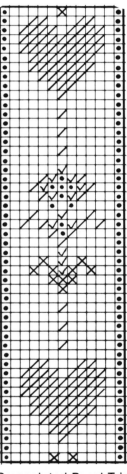

Grospointed Panel Trim

"Stencilled" Fabric for a Child's Room

A whimsical design "stencilled" with washable permanent acrylic paint onto a length of sheeting or muslin or any other fabric makes for fun in a child's room. Our allover pattern has multicolored letters of the alphabet in two different sizes stencilled, at random, onto a length of fiberglass, with little bunny-head balloons interspersed between the letters. We used our special "designer" fabric as broad stripes on a child's bedspread and matching cafe curtains, although it could be used as well to make a pillow cover, a slipcover for a chair or a toy chest, a pattern on a lampshade, or a blanket and coordinated wall hanging.

Materials:
tracing paper
2 sets stencil lettering guides, one 2 inches and one 4 inches
manicure or decoupage scissors
straight pins
washable fabric, in a solid color
acrylic tube paints, in yellow, light green, orange, royal blue, and white
artist's fine paintbrush
cardboard
felt-tipped marking pen, in permanent black

The Fabric

Trace onto paper letters from both the 2-inch and 4-inch stencil guides, the number that you trace depending on the size of the piece of fabric to be decorated. Then trace a number of the bunny-head balloons from the illustration (eliminating the string), the number of these also depending on the size of the fabric. Cut out the paper tracings and pin them to the fabric, in this way establishing a pattern, with both the letters and the balloons placed at random or in any other arrangement you might prefer. Using the white paint for a base coat and the paintbrush, paint the letters you've chosen on the fabric, painting directly through the openings on the stencil guides and removing the paper markers as you work. When the letters have all been painted, trace one more balloon, this time on cardboard. Cut out this tracing and, using it as a pattern, trace around it on the fabric, using the marking pen to trace with and again removing the "positioning" paper markers as you work. Finally, paint the balloons white, being careful to stay within the marking-pen outlines. When the paint has dried thoroughly, apply a second coat, using our choice of colors or your own for the letters and white once more for the balloons, filling in the entire space within the marking-pen outline for the balloons. Now trace the bunny eyes onto your original cardboard pattern for the balloons, cut out these openings, and with the marking pen draw the outline of these openings onto the heads. Finally, draw in the eyeballs, the nose, the mouth, and the string, working freehand with the marking pen. Then outline each of the alphabet letters with the same black pen.

Filet Mesh Cafe Curtains

These crocheted cafes and the matching valance, crisp and white, are worked in an open mesh and then edged with full, richly textured popcorn-stitch ruffles. Charming in a colonial, French provincial, or very modern setting, ours were designed to touch the sill of a window with an inside measurement of 29 inches in width and 41 inches in length. Instructions are given, along with those for ours, for adjusting the size to meet your own particular specifications.

Materials:
13 balls (100 yards each) Coats and Clark's "Speed-Cro-Sheen," in white
aluminum crochet hook, size F
needle and thread, in white
2 expansion curtain rods, about 1 inch in diameter

Filet Mesh Pattern Stitch (multiple of 3 ch plus 1): *Row 1:* Ch 5, 1 dc in sixth ch from hook, *ch 2, sk 2 ch, 1 dc in next ch, rep from * across, ch 5, and turn.

Row 2: Sk first dc, *1 dc in the next dc, ch 2, sk 2 ch, rep from * across and end with 1 dc in the third ch of the turning ch-5 of the previous row, ch 5, and turn. Repeat Row 2 for pattern.

Popcorn Pattern Stitch (multiple of 11): *Row 1:* Ch 2, dc in fourth ch from hook and in each of the next 3 ch, *5 dc in the next ch, drop the lp from the hook, insert hook in the first dc of the 5-dc group, pick up the lp and pull it through (one popcorn made), 1 dc in each of the next 5 ch, rep from * across, ch 1, and turn. *Row 2:* Work 1 sc in each dc and in each popcorn across, and end 1 sc in second ch of starting ch-2, ch 2, and turn. *Row 3:* Sk the first sc, 1 dc in the next sc, *popcorn in the next sc, 1 dc in each of the next 5 sc, rep from * across and end with 1 dc in each of the last 2 sc, ch 1, and turn. *Row 4:* Repeat Row 2. *Row 5:* Sk first sc, *1 dc in each of the next 4 sc, popcorn in the next sc, rep from * across, and end with 1 dc in each of the last 5 sc, ch 1, and turn. *Row 6:* Repeat Row 2. Repeat Rows 3 through 6 for pattern.

Gauge in Single Crochet: 6 stitches = 1 inch

The Curtains

Lower panels (Make two): For the filet mesh portion, ch 70 (or any multiple of 3 ch plus 1 for the desired size of 2¾ inches less than half the width of your window). Follow the pattern for that stitch until piece measures 16 inches (or 4½ inches less than the desired length from the point at which you hang your cafe rod). Fasten off. For the popcorn ruffled portion, ch 253 (or any multiple of 11 ch that is 1½ times the length of one long and one short edge of the curtain). Follow the popcorn pattern until piece measures 2½ inches. Fasten off and then make another piece in the same manner for the other panel. Now draw thread tightly through the starting chains to gather these two pieces so that each one will fit, evenly ruffled, down one long edge and across the bound-off edge of one of the panels. Sew the ruffles to the panels along what will now become the inside and bottom edges. Work 2 rows of sc up the remaining long outside edge and across the top of each panel, continuing the top 2 rows of sc across the top of the inside ruffle too.

Tabs (Make ten): Ch 7 and work in sc on 6 sts for 4 inches. Fasten off. Fold the tabs in half and sew five of them evenly spaced across the top of each panel, as shown in the photograph.

Valance: Ch 175 (or any multiple of 3 ch plus 1 for the exact width of your window). Work even in sc for 1½ inches and then work 3 rows of the filet mesh pattern. Fasten off. For the popcorn ruffled portion, ch 264 (or any multiple of 11 ch that is 1½ times the width of the start of the valance). Work in the popcorn-pattern stitch for 2½ inches and fasten off. Draw thread tightly through the starting chain of this piece to gather it into a ruffle that will fit across the last filet mesh row of the valance; sew it in place. Now with the wrong side of the work facing, work a casing for the top rod as follows: Attach yarn to the right top end of the 1½-inch sc portion of the valance, *ch 8, sl st at the bottom of the sc rows approximately 1 inch beyond the last st at the top, ch 8, sl st at the top of the sc rows approximately 1 inch beyond the last st, and rep from * across the row, ending with a sl st at either the top or bottom of the last st, depending on the number of sts involved. Fasten off.

Lacy Knitted Curtains

A sheer yarn worked in the simple stockinette stitch on large #13 needles gives a peek-a-boo, see-through effect to these curtains. The color pattern is a striped one combining three different soft hues. Designed with a valance between two side panels, this window dressing is rather Victorian in flavor, although it could very conceivably make a strong statement in any modern home or in one that is eclectic in style, combining the very best of all periods to achieve a particular mood and setting. Our curtains, with the joined valance, were designed to fit a double window measuring about 48 inches to the sill and about 72 inches wide, although the instructions offer suggestions as to how you can adjust them to fit your own window or windows.

Materials:
5 balls (1½ ounces each) Reynolds Kali Mousse in wheat (A), 5 balls in
 white (B), and 6 balls in medium blue (C)
1 pair straight knitting needles, # 13
aluminum crochet hook, size G
yarn needle

Gauge in Stockinette Stitch: 2 stitches = 1 inch

4 rows = 1 inch

The Curtains

Left side panel: With A, cast on 104 sts or the number of sts, calculated at the gauge of 2 sts to 1 inch, that will equal in inches the length of the finished curtain you plan to make plus an additional 8 sts to make a casing at the top. Working in a color-stripe pattern of *4 rows A, 2 rows B, 2 rows C, and 2 rows B and repeating from the * throughout, work even in stockinette stitch for 24 rows, adding or subtracting 2 rows for every inch that your window measurement is wider or narrower than our 72-inch window. *At the beginning of the next k row, dec 1 st, work even to the end of the row, and dec 1 st at the end of the following p row. Repeat from *, decreasing 1 st at the same edge of every row until 20 sts remain, being certain that the piece ends with the fourth row of A. If the striped pattern does not end in this way because of the number of stripes you need for the particular size panel you are making, compensate by adding as many rows as necessary on the 20 sts. Bind off.

Right side panel: Work as for the left side panel, reversing the shaping and starting by casting on 20 sts with color A. Work as many rows as you did on the 20 sts for the first panel and then increase at the same bottom end on every row until there are 104 sts. End the piece with 24 rows even on these 104 sts or the same number of even rows as were used to start the first panel, and bind off.

Center valance: With A, cast on 20 sts. Working in the striped pattern as for the side panels, work even for 2 inches. Then inc 1 st at the end of the next k row (for the bottom edge) and rep this inc every 2 inches until there are 30 sts. Work even on these sts for 38 inches. Then dec 1 st, again at the same edge, every 2 inches until 20 sts remain. Work even on 20 sts for about 2 inches, ending with 4 rows of A. Bind off.

Finishing: Join each end of the center valance with each short end of the side panels by sewing them together with an overcast stitch. Then turn under 2 inches of the top of the piece to make a rod casing and hem in place. Finally, make a crocheted edging long enough to fit around the side panels and the valance, measuring across the straight bottom portion and the inside edges of both panels and along the bottom of the valance. Work this edging in the following way: With C, crochet a chain to measure the necessary length, making this chain in any multiple of 7 sts plus 5. Then work as follows: Ch 1, 1 sc in the second ch from hook, 1 sc in each of the next 2 ch, *ch 4, 1 sc in the fourth ch from hook (picot made), 1 sc in each of the next 2 ch, ch 9, turn, skip the (2 sc, 1 picot, and 2 sc) just made, 1 sc in the next sc, turn, 13 sc in the ch-9 sp, 1 sc in each of the next 5 ch of the foundation chain, rep from * across, and end the last rep with 13 sc in the last ch-9 sp. Fasten off. Overcast the edging now to the parts of the curtains and valance to be trimmed.

Casement Cloth by the Yard

Delicate strips of hairpin lace are joined together here with crochet stitches to make a stunning piece of material especially suitable for a curtain or drapery window dressing. Each individual strip is 4 inches wide, including a final edging of single crochet along each side edge to finish the loops of the hairpin lace. In designing the cloth, we've alternated the joining of the strips with solid 2-inch-wide bands of single crochet and 1½-inch bands of crochet worked in a lacy zigzag pattern. The size of the piece of fabric you make is up to you, depending on your needs. To increase its size, you need only to follow our instructions, continuing with the work on the loom for the desired length, and to make as many additional strips (following our alternating joining pattern, which means that you must make an even number of strips) as you need for the width. You might even try hanging the completed strips horizontally; in this case you would, of course, need to adjust the number of strips you make and the length of each one.

Materials:
4 skeins (3½ ounces each) Red Heart Sparkling Knitting Worsted Type Yarn
  (for a piece of cloth approximately 33 × 50 inches), in sea foam
adjustable hairpin-lace loom
aluminum crochet hook, size K
tapestry needle, #18
needle and thread, in light green

Gauge in Single Crochet: 3 stitches = 1 inch

The Cloth

Hairpin-lace strips: With the loom adjusted to 4 inches, make six strips with 146 lps on each side of each strip, or the number of loops necessary to reach your desired length. Finish each long side of each strip as follows: With right side of work facing, *sc through 2 lps tog, ch 1, rep from * across, and end with 1 sc through the last 2 lps, ch 2, and turn. Next row: Work 1 sc in second ch from hook, in each ch-1 lp, and in each sc across. Fasten off.

Joining the strips: Joining A: Holding two finished strips together with the right side of the work facing, attach yarn to the top of one strip and work 1 sl st in the first sc on that strip, then ch 5, sk 3 sc on the top of the second strip, sl st in the fourth sc on that strip, *ch 5, sk the next 3 sc on the first strip, sl st in the next sc, ch 5, sk the next 3 sc on the second strip, sl st in the next sc, rep from * for the full length of the two strips being joined. Joining B: Work 2 rows of sc along the outer edge of one of the joined strips, working 1 sc in each sc along the row. Then work 2 rows of sc along the edge of the next strip to be joined. Finally, sew the strips together with an overcast stitch.

Finishing: Continue in this manner to join the strips, alternating throughout an A joining with a B joining and using an A joining to connect the last two strips. To finish the piece of material, work 2 additional rows of sc along the outermost left and right edges of the piece. Then crochet 3 rows of sc across the width as follows, to make a border for the bottom edge: With the right side of the work facing, work 1 sc in each of the first 4 sc border rows, ch 4, 1 sc in the spine, ch 4, 1 sc in each of the next 2 sc rows, ch 4 across the next A joining, and continue in this manner across the width of the piece, working 1 sc in each spine and in each sc row across and a ch-4 between all the sc and spine sts and across all A joining spaces. End by working 1 sc in each of the last 4 sc border rows, then ch 1, and turn. Work 2 more rows of sc now, working 1 sc in each sc and in each ch st across the first row and 1 sc in each sc on the second row. Fasten off. To finish the top of the piece for hanging, work in the same manner as for the bottom to the point at which the sc rows have been completed. Then work a row of sc through the back lps of the sts only for a turn-under and finally 3 additional rows of sc in the usual manner; fasten off. Then fold the additional 3 rows to the wrong side of the work and hem the last row in place to make a casing.

Unusual Woven Inserts for Prefabricated Shutter Frames

A three-color striped crocheted pattern, woven through both horizontally and vertically with two other colors, becomes a handsome fabric to be inserted within the openings of unfinished wooden shutter frames. Further texture has been added to this fabric by using four different materials to make it, including a soft mohair yarn, a four-ply knitting worsted, a bulky yarn, and some medium-width rickrack. Our pieces were made to measure 12 by 30 inches, but the fabric you make can easily be made longer and/or wider to fit whatever dimensions your shutter frames require.

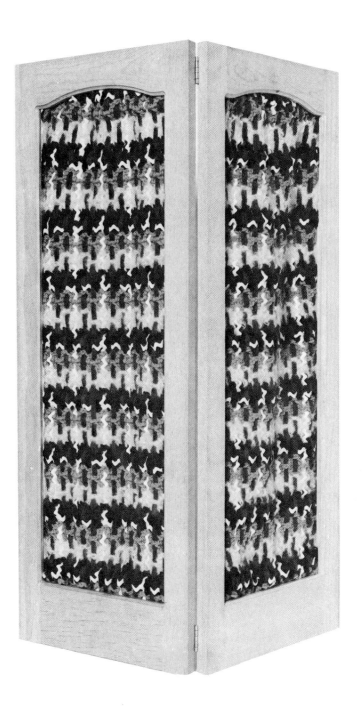

Materials:
3 balls (1 ounce each) Columbia-Minerva Reverie, in off-white (A)
5 skeins (2 ounces each) Columbia-Minerva Nantuk Bulky in wood brown (B)
  and 3 skeins in copperglo (C)
2 skeins (4 ounces each) Columbia-Minerva 4-ply knitting worsted, in
  new camel (D)
40 yards medium-width rickrack, in white
aluminum crochet hook, size K
needle and thread, in natural
1½ yards blanket binding, 2 inches wide, in dark brown
8 small extension curtain rods with hooks

Pattern Stitch: *Row 1:* Ch 4, dc in fifth ch from hook, *ch 1, sk 1 ch, dc in the next ch, rep from * across the row and end with 1 dc in the last ch, ch 3, and turn. *Row 2:* *Sk 1 dc, dc in the next dc, ch 1, rep from * across the row and end with 1 dc in the third ch of the starting ch-4, ch 3, and turn. *Row 3:* *Sk 1 dc, dc in the next dc, ch 1, rep from * across the row and end with 1 dc in the second of the turning ch-3, ch 3, and turn. Repeat Row 3 throughout the pattern.

Gauge in Pattern Stitch: 4 double crochet and 3 spaces = 2 inches
3 rows = 2 inches

The Inserts

Make four pieces: With A, ch 33. Work even in pat, alternating 2 rows A, 2 rows D, and 2 rows B until a tenth 2-row stripe of A has been completed; fasten off. The piece should measure approximately 32 inches. Starting at one side edge, weaving vertically and alternating the over-and-under weaving process along each line of weaving, *weave 2 rows with double strands of C, then 1 row with rickrack, and rep from * across the piece, ending with 2 rows of C. Tack the start and end of each woven stripe in place on the wrong side of the finished piece. Now weave horizontally with the rickrack only, again alternating the over-and-under weaving process and weaving only through the first of each 2-row color-B stripe. When these stripes have been woven, again tack them securely on each end.

Finishing: Work 1 row of color-over-color sc around the four sides of each panel, working a sufficient number of sts so that the edges lie flat and 3 sc in each corner st as you turn. Finally, cut the blanket binding into strips long enough to fit across the top and bottom of each panel, and sew the strips in place. Insert the rods through the binding and hang them on hooks attached to the back of each shutter frame, thus using the rods to stretch the woven pieces.

A Pasta-Beaded Macramé Curtain

Worked in a natural-colored bulky yarn, a series of simple macramé knots strung with 5½-inch-long manicotti enameled a brilliant blue makes for a most unusual window or wall treatment. (It could also be used as a room divider.) Our finished hanging, which is worked in three panels, measures 5 feet wide and 8 feet long, and it required sixteen 4-ounce skeins of yarn and three standard-size boxes of manicotti to make it. You can alter the size of the piece as you wish by varying the length of each working cord and the number of cords used for each panel. The choice of the colors you use for your own piece is up to you, too. Green yarn and white enameled pasta would be a stunning combination for a summer or tropical home, while shades of yellow, gold, and orange would add a note of sunshine to any setting.

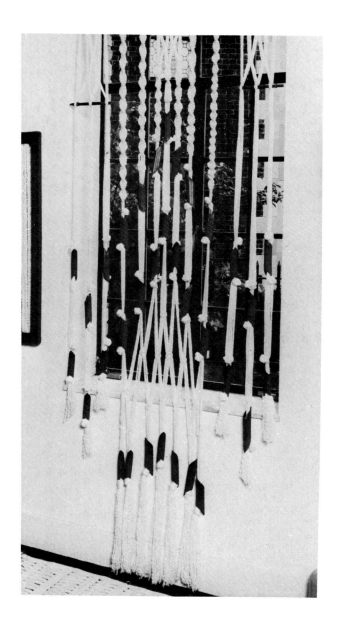

Materials:
3 boxes (14 pieces per box) #21 manicotti
1 spray can (13 ounces) enamel, in bright blue
16 skeins (4 ounces each) Bernat Berella Bulky, in natural
1 expansion curtain rod, 60 inches long
rubber bands

The Curtain

Spread thirty-three of the manicotti over newspaper, spray them with the enamel, and allow to dry. Turn them to an unpainted portion, spray as before, and let dry. Continue to do this until all sides have been covered. Now start the curtain.

Center portion: Cut twenty-eight strands of yarn, each 40 feet long. Arrange the strands into seven groups of four strands each, fold each group in half, and with the curtain rod hung at arm level, attach each of the folded seven groups to the rod with a lark's-head knot, spacing each knot and each group 4 inches apart on the rod. There are now fifty-six strands hanging from the rod. To prevent the strands from becoming tangled, roll each group of cords into a small ball and secure the ball with a rubber band. Following the chart, work to completion a lattice pattern of alternating square knots, using for each knot four filler cords and four working cords, two on either side of the filler. For the first row of square knots, use four strands from one group of eight strands and four strands from the adjacent group. On the next row, alternate this. Continuing with the pattern and using each group of eight strands for a half-square-knot sinnet, make seven of these sinnets, using the two outer strands on each side of each group as the working cords and the center four strands of eight as the filler and working each sinnet to the length indicated on the chart. Periodically raising the rod to make for a more comfortable working position, continue as follows: Leave 1 inch of the strands at the bottom of each sinnet hanging free. Then on each of the seven sinnets, *make one square-knot button, thread one piece of pasta onto the eight strands below the button, and make another square-knot button just below the pasta.* Now leave 10 inches more unworked (combing the strands so that they are straight, smooth, and even) and rep the procedure between *'s. There are now fourteen "beads" strung onto the center portion of the curtain. Working on the middle group of the eight strands only now, leave 10 inches unworked, work one square knot, and then follow the chart for the working of the second knotted lattice design to completion. There are now again fifty-six free hanging strands. Leaving 4 inches unworked on each group of eight strands, again as shown on the chart, thread one piece of pasta through all eight strands of each group. Then make a slipknot just underneath each piece of pasta. Finally, trim the remaining strands of the center portion of the curtain to measure an even 8 feet from top to bottom. Then unravel the end of each strand so that the three plies of the yarn are separated and there is a curly look to the bottom strands.

Side portions (Make two): Cut twelve strands of yarn, each 25 feet long. Fold these strands in half. Then with a lark's-head knot, attach three groups of four strands each onto one end of the rod, spacing them 4 inches apart and 4 inches out from either side of the center panel. Now work the lattice design on each of these panels as indicated on the chart. Then on the two outer groups of

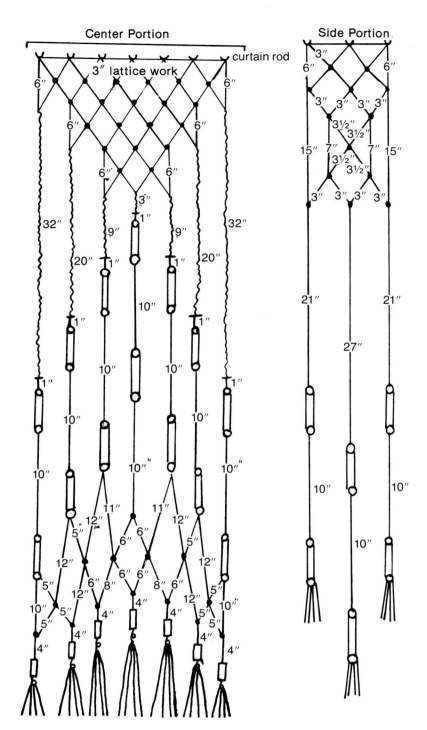

Center Portion

Side Portion

curtain rod

3" lattice work

Knot Key:
| = unworked strands
∪ = lark's-head knot
• = square knot
⟨ = half-square-knot sinnet
○ = square-knot button
▯ = manicotti
ϵ = slipknot
⋀ = fringe

eight strands, leave 21 inches unworked and rep from between *'s as on the center panel. On the center group of each side panel, leave 27 inches unworked and then rep from between *'s as on the center panel. Leave 10 inches unworked now on each of the three groups of each side panel, and rep from between *'s of center panel once more. Finally, trim the remaining loose strands to 4 inches below the last square-knot button and unravel the ends as on the center panel. If desired, complete each side panel by inserting a 1-inch-in-diameter bundle of painted spaghetti, approximately 2 inches wider than the side panel, through the last three square knots of the top lattice-work portion.

DECORATIVE ACCESSORIES

Percival, A Life-Size Life-Time Friend

Crocheted with a large hook and double strands of yarn, Percival is a rabbit just about four feet tall who would be happy to be a constant friend and companion to any child. Dressed in a sailor suit and cap, he also sports a "hidden" pocket for storing a child's most precious things.

Materials:

9 skeins (4 ounces each) Spinnerin 4-ply Orlon acrylic in aqua (MC), 3 skeins in white (A), and 1 skein each in black (B) and orange (C)

aluminum crochet hook, size K

medium-weight cardboard, 18 inches square

stuffing material, including all the pieces from your scrap bag plus two 1-pound bags Polyfil

wool needle or tapestry needle, #18

white glue

1 piece felt, 2 inches square, in red

6 straight pins with white heads (for the eyeballs)

Gauge in Single Crochet: 5 stitches = 2 inches, using double strands of yarn

Percival

Shoes: Working in sc with double strands of yarn throughout, make two pieces as follows: For each shoe, ch 21 with B. Work even on 20 sts for 8 inches and fasten off. Fold the piece in half lengthwise and place the fold so that it becomes the center of the sole of the shoe. Then sew together the first 9 sts of the top opening to make the instep. To complete the shoe, attach B again, and with the right side facing, work across 11 sts on one side of the opening above the instep and then continue across the 11 sts on the other side. Work back and forth on these 22 sts for 4 rows and fasten off.

Legs and torso: Work along the top of each shoe as follows: Sk the last 5 sts worked at the top of the shoe, attach MC, sc across the remaining 17 sts, and end the row by working across the 5 skipped sts at the beginning, ch 1, and turn (22 sts). Next row: *Sc in the next sc, 2 sc in the next, rep from * across, ch 1, and turn (33 sts). Next row: *Sc in each of the next 2 sc, 2 sc in the next sc, rep from * across, ch 1, and turn (44 sts). Continue in this manner to inc 11 sts evenly spaced on each rnd, having 1 st more between each pt of inc, until there are 66 sts. Work even on the 66 sts for 4 rows and then dec as follows: Next row: *Sc in each of the next 4 sc, work 2 tog (1 dec), rep from * across, ch 1, and turn (55 sts). Work 2 rows even. Next row: *Sc in each of the next 3 sc, dec 1, rep from * across, ch 1, and turn (44 sts). Work 2 rows even. Next row: *Sc in each of the next 2 sc, dec 1, rep from * across, ch 1, and turn (33 sts). Work even now on 33 sts until 18 inches in all have been worked, ending with a wrong-side row. Next row: Sl st across 2 sts, sc to within the last 2 sts, ch 1, and turn. Now work on 29 sts for 15 inches, ending at the front edge. Then shape the neck: Dec 1 st at beg of the next row, work even to the end of the row, ch 1, and turn. Next row: Work even. Rep the last 2 rows 5 times more. Finally, work even on 23 sts for 2 rows and fasten off.

Paws and arms (Make two): With A, ch 2, work 5 sc in the second ch from hook. Do not turn but, working around, on the next rnd work 2 sc in each sc (10 sts). Next rnd: *Sc in the next sc, 2 sc in the next sc, rep from * around (15 sts). Next rnd: *Sc in each of the next 2 sc, 2 sc in the next sc, rep from * around (20 sts). Work even until piece measures 5 inches. Fasten off A, attach MC, and work 1 sc in each sc around, ch 1, and turn. Working back and forth now, work as follows: Next row: *Sc in the next sc, 2 sc in the next sc, rep from

* across, ch 1, and turn (30 sts). Next row: *Sc in each of the next 2 sc, 2 sc in the next sc, rep from * across, ch 1, and turn (40 sts). Work 2 rows even. Next row: *Sc in each of the next 3 sc, work 2 tog (1 dec), rep from * across, ch 1, and turn (32 sts). Work 2 rows even. Next row: *Sc in each of the next 2 sc, work 2 tog, rep from * across (24 sts). Work even now on 24 sts for 14 inches. Fasten off.

Neck insert: To make the front, ch 3 with A. Work 1 sc in the second ch from hook, 1 sc in the next ch, ch 1, and turn. Work 1 row even on 2 sts. Then inc 1 st at beg and end of the next row and every other row until there are 12 sts. Work 3 rows even. For one half of the back, work across the first 6 sts for 3 rows and fasten off; for the other half of the back, attach yarn in the seventh st, work across the remaining 6 sts for 3 rows, and fasten off.

Head: With A, ch 2, work 5 sc in the second st from hook and then, continuing around, work as follows: Next rnd: Work 2 sc in each sc around (10 sts). Next rnd: *Sc in the next sc, 2 sc in the next sc, rep from * around (15 sts). Next rnd: *Sc in each of the next 2 sc, 2 sc in the next sc, rep from * around (20 sts). Continue in this manner to inc 5 sts evenly spaced on each rnd, adding 1 st more between each pt of inc, until there are 90 sts. Work even for 4 rnds and then dec as follows: Next rnd: *Sc in each of the next 16 sc, work 2 tog (1 dec), rep from * around (85 sts). Next rnd: *Sc in each of the next 15 sc, dec 1, rep from * around (80 sts). Continue in this manner to dec 5 sts evenly spaced on each rnd, having 1 st less between each pt of dec, until 40 sts remain. Now dec 1 st in every st until the piece is closed, at the same time stuffing the entire head firmly with the Polyfil as you work and starting the stuffing process at the point where there are 40 sts. When all sts are gone, fasten off.

Ears (Make four): With A, ch 9 and then work even back and forth on 8 sts for 4 inches. Dec 1 st at beg and end of the next row and then work even for 4 inches more. Rep the dec row, work even for 3 inches, rep the dec row once more, work even for 1 inch, and fasten off.

Hat: With MC, ch 2, work 6 sc in the second st from hook and, continuing to work around, work as follows: Next rnd: Work 2 sc in each sc around (12 sts). Next rnd: *Sc in the next sc, 2 sc in the next sc, rep from * around (18 sc). Next rnd: *Sc in each of the next 2 sc, 2 sc in the next sc, rep from * around (24 sc). Continue in this manner to inc 6 sts evenly spaced on every rnd, having 1 st more between each pt of inc, until there are 42 sts. Work 3 rnds even. Next rnd: *Sc in the next sc, 2 sc in the next sc, and rep from * around (63 sts). Work even for 6 rnds and fasten off.

Collar and bow: With MC, ch 23 for the collar. Then work back and forth even on 22 sts for 5 inches, ending with a wrong-side row. Next row: Work in sc across 6 sts, ch 1, and turn. Next row: Work 2 tog, work 1 sc in each of the next 4 sc, ch 1, and turn (5 sts). Next row: Work across 3 sts, work 2 tog, ch 1, and turn (4 sts). Work 3 rows even. Next row: Work across 2 sts, work 2 tog, ch 1, and turn (3 sts). Work even for 3 rows. Next row: Work 1 sc, work 2 tog, ch 1, and turn (2 sts). Work even for 3 rows. Next row: Work 2 tog, ch 1, and turn (1 st). Work even on the 1 st for 3 rows and fasten off. To complete the collar, sk the center 10 sts on the last row where 22 sts were worked, attach MC again, and work across the remaining 6 sts to correspond to the last 6 sts worked, reversing the shaping. Finally, work 1 row of sc around the completed collar,

68

working 3 sc in each corner st as you turn. For the bow, ch 31 with C and then work even on 30 sts for 2 rows and fasten off.

Back pocket: With MC, ch 19 and then work even on 18 sts for 8 inches, ending with a wrong-side row. Do not break off yarn, but work 1 rnd of sc around the entire outer edge of the piece, working 3 sc in each corner st as you turn.

Finishing: Stuffing the pieces firmly as you sew the various seams and using scraps for the bulk of the filler and the Polyfil around the scraps to give an even, smooth look to the stuffed portions, work as follows: Sew together the toe and heel seams of the shoes, the inner seams of both legs, and the center front and back body seams. Sew the neck insert to the top of the body. Now stuff the paws and the arms and sew together the arm seams. Sew one arm in position to each side of the body, as shown in the photograph. Then sew on the head, using the part that was closed last as the back of the head. Cut two pieces of cardboard to the shape of the ears, lay each piece between two ear pieces, sew the crocheted pieces together over the cardboard, and sew the finished ears to the sides of the top of the head. Stuff the hat lightly and sew it on between the ears. Sew the collar in place; knot the bow in the center and sew it in place. Sew the pocket to the center of the back, placing the bottom of the pocket just above the waistband and stitching the bottom and two sides only. Now, make a head support band with A by working back and forth in sc on 3 sts for 5 inches. Sew this band tightly around the top of the neck just below the head. With double strands of C, make two chains for the shoelaces, each 8 inches long; with double strands of MC, make one for the waistband that is 28 inches long; with double strands of A, make one for part of the chevron that is 15 inches long and another with C to the same length; with double strands of A, make one for part of the collar that is 38 inches long and another with C to the same length; with double strands of A, make one for the hat that is 12 inches long and another with C to the same length. Sew all the finished chains in place. Finally, with B, make the following chains to establish Percival's features: two, each 2 inches long, for the eyebrows; two, each 2 inches long, for the eyes; one approximately 2 inches long for the the portion between the nose and the mouth, and a last one 6 inches long for the mouth. Glue these pieces in place and then finish the face as follows: For the nose, ch 6 with B, join with a sl st to form a ring, and then work 12 sc in the center of the ring; fasten off. Glue the nose in place. Cut six strands of B yarn for the whiskers, each 8 inches long, and glue them in place. For the tongue, cut a semicircle of the felt and glue it in place below the mouth. Stick three of each of the six pins at the bottom of each eye for eyeballs and glue them securely in place.

A Hairpin-Lace Wall Hanging Trimmed with Dried Flowers, p. 21; Lacy Knitted Curtains, p. 56; Granny Squares under Glass, p. 74.

73

Granny Squares under Glass

A few old-fashioned crocheted granny squares joined together and covered with clear glass form the unusual decoration for the top of the lamp table shown in the color photograph. The look is a quaint and charming one, rather Victorian in flavor, and it is an easy one to accomplish. Although our piece was made to cover a table with a 16¾-inch square top, there are many ways in which you can vary the size to fit the top of a particular table of your own. One suggestion for doing this might be to double the finished piece widthwise before the final trimming has been added, in this way making a rectangle that measures approximately 16¾ by 33½ inches. Doubling the piece both width-wise and lengthwise for a finished square measuring 33½ by 33½ inches would be another way of changing the size; and still another would be to add rows of single crochet, in the final trimming color and in any direction, around the outer edge of our square, again before the trim has been added.

Materials:
2 balls (1½ ounces each) Reynolds Kali Mousse in medium blue (A), 1 ball in white (B), and 2 balls in wheat (C)
aluminum crochet hook, size F
needle and thread, in white

Gauge in Double Crochet: 9 stitches = 2 inches

6 rows = 1 inch

The Cover

Granny squares (Make eight): With A, ch 6 and join with a sl st to form a ring. Rnd 1: Ch 3, 2 dc in the ring, (ch 1, 3 dc in the ring) 3 times, ch 1, join with a sl st to the third st of the starting ch-3. Fasten off A. Rnd 2: Attach B to any ch-1 sp, ch 3, work 2 dc, ch 1, and 3 dc in the same sp (corner), *ch 1, work 3 dc, ch 1, and 3 dc in the next sp (another corner), rep from * twice more, ch 1, and join with a sl st to the third st of the starting ch-3. Rnd 3: Sl st in each of the next 2 dc, sl st in the next ch-1 sp, ch 3, work 2 dc, ch 1, and 3 dc in the same sp (corner), *ch 1, 3 dc in the next ch-1 sp, ch 1, corner in the next corner sp, rep from * twice more, ch 1, 3 dc in the next sp, ch 1, and join with a sl st in the third st of the starting ch-3. Rnd 4: Sl st in each of the next 2 dc, sl st in the next ch-1 sp, ch 3, work 2 dc, ch 1, and 3 dc in the same sp (corner), *(ch 1, 3 dc in the next ch-1 sp) twice, ch 1, corner in the next corner, rep from * twice more, (ch 1, 3 dc in the next sp) twice, ch1, and join with a sl st in the third st of the starting ch-3. Fasten off.

Make a large square now from four of the smaller ones by sewing together their edges. (Use a needle and thread for this part of the work because of the nubby quality of the yarn.) Now attach C in any corner ch-1 sp, ch 3, work 2 dc, ch 1, and 3 dc in the same sp (corner), *(ch 1, 3 dc in the next ch-1 sp) 8 times, ch 1, work another corner, rep from * twice more, then (ch 1, 3 dc in the next ch-1 sp) 8 times, ch 1, and join this rnd with a sl st to the third st of the starting ch-3. Fasten off. Attach A and rep the last rnd once more, repeating the portion within parentheses 9 times instead of 8 times. Fasten off. Now work around each of the four sides of this large square as follows: Attach C in any corner sp, ch 3, *work 1 dc between the first and second dc of the next group of 3 dc on the previous rnd, 1 dc between the second and third dc of the same group, 1 dc in the next ch-1 sp, rep from * ten times more (34 dc on the row, including the first ch-3). Ch 3 and turn at the end of the row. Then work in dc on 34 sts for 6 more rows and fasten off. Repeat these 7 rows on each of the other three sides of the large square. Then sew one of each of the remaining four small squares in place in the four free corners extending beyond the dc rows that were worked with C.

Finishing: Make an edging around the four sides of the square as follows: Rnd 1: Attach A in a st that is 3 sts before any corner ch-1 sp, sl st in the same st, work 1 sc in each of the next 2 sts, sc in the next ch-1 sp, ch 4, sc in the same ch-1 sp (corner picot made), *work 1 sc in each of the next 4 sts, ch 4, 1 sc in the next st (picot), rep from * around, being sure to space your sts so that a corner picot can be worked in each of the remaining three corners. Join the end of the rnd with a sl st in the first sl st. Rnd 2: Work 1 sl st in the next st, ch 9, sk the corner picot and work 1 sc in the second sc after the picot, *ch 9, sk 2 sc and the picot, sc in the second sc after the picot, rep from * around, joining the rnd with a sl st in the first sl st. Rnd 3: Ch 1, *work 9 sc in each ch-9 lp, sl st in the next sc, rep from * around, and end with a sl st in the first ch-1. Fasten off. Finally, block the finished piece and place it under glass on the table with the color-A edging either covered by or extending beyond the glass.

Elegant Table Accessories

Silver and gold threads and a small amount of white synthetic yarn are the basic materials used to fashion this handsome table set of hot-plate mats, glass jackets, and napkin rings. Metallic strands woven through a crocheted mesh background form the design. Since even the metallic threads are, in addition to being tarnish-proof, completely hand-washable, the set is practical as well as attractive.

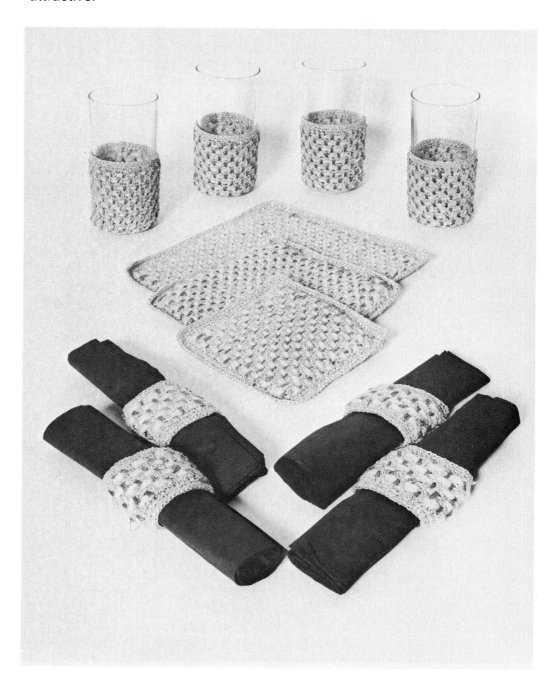

Materials:
5 balls (1 ounce each) Columbia-Minerva Camelot in silver (A) and
    2 balls in gold (B)
1 skein (4 ounces) Columbia-Minerva Civona, in white (C)
aluminum crochet hook, size E
tapestry needle, #18
needle and thread, in a neutral color
¼ yard washable lining material, in a neutral color

Pattern Stitch: *Row 1:* Hdc in the second ch from hook, *ch 1, sk 1 ch, hdc in the next ch, rep from * across the row and end with 1 hdc in the last ch, ch 3, and turn. *Row 2:* Sk 1 hdc, *hdc in the next hdc, ch 1, rep from * across the row and end with 1 hdc in the last hdc, ch 3, and turn. *Row 3:* Sk 1 hdc, *hdc in the next hdc, ch 1, rep from * across the row, and end with 1 hdc in the turning ch of the previous row, ch 3, and turn. Repeat Row 3 for the pattern stitch.

Gauge in Pattern Stitch (unwoven): 8 stitches = 1 inch

Three Hot-Plate Mats

Instructions are written for the smallest square mat, woven and blocked to measure 5½ inches. Changes for the 8-inch and the 10-inch mats are in parentheses.

    With A, ch 36 (56, 72). Work even in pat st until the piece measures 4½ (7, 9) inches square and then fasten off. Weave each piece as follows: Cut two strands of B yarn, each 3 inches longer than the crocheted square they are to be woven through. Then, using the tapestry needle, weave the strands over and under through the holes of the pattern stitch vertically, leaving 1½ inches of the yarn extending at each end. Repeat this process for a second row, alternating the weaving on this row. Continue in this way until all the vertical rows have been woven. Then with double strands of C, weave the horizontal rows, again alternating the pattern on each row and working the design so that the C strands are woven under the B strands.

    Finishing: When the mats have been completely woven and there are approximately 1½ inches of the weaving threads extending on all four sides of each one, tack these ends in place with needle and thread in order to keep the weaving firmly in position. Then cut a piece of lining material slightly larger than each piece, turn under the edges, and sew it on, covering the tacked weaving threads on the underside. Finally, with A work 3 rows of sc around the outer edges of the mats, working a sufficient number of sts so that the piece lies flat and working 3 sc in each corner st as you turn.

Four Glass Jackets

These jackets were designed for 8-ounce glasses measuring 6 inches high and 2¾ inches in diameter across the top, although there is sufficient stretch to the finished pieces to enable them to be fitted over glasses of other sizes.

    Starting at the bottom with A, ch 4 and join with a sl st to form a ring. Next rnd: Work 6 sc in the center of the ring. Next rnd: Work 2 sc in each sc around

(12 sc). Next rnd: *Work 1 sc in each of the first 2 sc, 2 sc in the next sc, rep from * around (18 sc). Continue now to inc 6 sts evenly spaced on each rnd, having 1 st more between each pt of inc, until there are 36 sts. Fasten off. To make the top of the jacket, ch 38 with A. Work even in pat st for 3 inches and fasten off. Weave this top portion in the same manner now as the mats were woven, with this difference: When working with the color-B vertical strands, leave 1½ inches excess yarn at one end only (this will become the bottom), weave up to the top, then down again to the bottom, and cut the ends, again leaving 1½ inches free. Rep this process across the entire piece. The horizontal color-C strands are woven in exactly the same manner as for the mats.

Finishing: Sew the two short ends of the top together. Then turn the finished piece to the wrong side, knot the ends of the free color-C strands securely together, and clip them closely. Sew the top piece to the bottom now, wrong sides together, letting the free color-B strands fall over to the wrong sides of the bottom circle. Tack these in place as for the mats, line the bottom to cover the tacked threads, and finally work 3 rnds of color-A sc around the top of each jacket, joining the last sc of the last round to the first sc of that round.

Four Napkin Rings

With A, ch 20. Then crochet and weave the piece as for the top of the glass jacket for 1¾ inches. Secure the free, hanging threads, line the ring, sew the two short ends together, and finally work 3 rounds of sc with A around both the top and bottom edges.

Soft Knitted Frills, Matching Inserts, and a Pillow to Trim Your Own Bedspread

An open, lacy knit stitch, worked in acrylic yarn on large needles, forms the soft and lovely trim on this charming bedspread. The fabric portion of the single-size spread itself was made to accommodate to the trim; in making your own piece, you can either start from scratch as we did, making it to any desired size, or cut a spread or coverlet that you already own into parts to which you can add the ruffles and inserts. A lacy pink bed pillow adds a little more yet to this lovely bed dressing.

Materials

25 skeins (1¾ ounces each) Unger Roly-Sport in pink for a single spread; 28 skeins for a double-size spread; 31 skeins for a queen-size spread; 34 skeins for a king-size spread; plus 4 skeins for a pillow

1 pair 14-inch knitting needles, #11, or a round needle the same size

2½ yards fabric for the single spread or the amount required to cover the top part of your bed (excluding the side drop), 45 inches wide, in pink and white stripes

6 yards lining fabric for the single-size spread plus ½ yard additional for each size larger, 48 inches wide, in white

needle and thread, in pink and in white

1 bag (1 pound) polyester stuffing material

Pattern Stitch: *Rows 1 and 2:* K. *Row 3:* K 1, *yo, k 1, rep from * across the row. *Row 4:* K, dropping the yo's of the previous row. Repeat Rows 1 through 4 for the pattern stitch.

Gauge: 5 stitches = 2 inches

The Spread

Inserts (Make two pieces): For the single spread, cast on 195 sts. K 1 row, then repeat Rows 1 through 4 twice, k 2 additional rows, and bind off. Make the inserts for other sizes in the same manner but repeat Rows 1 through 4 three times for the double size and four times for the queen and king sizes.

Ruffled tiers: For the sides of the spread, make six tiers in all on the same number of stitches for all sizes, two of which will be 8 inches, two 9 inches, and two 10 inches. To make the 8-inch tier, cast on 195 sts. K 1 row and then repeat Rows 1 through 4 until piece measures approximately 7½ inches, increasing 1 st in every other st on the first row only, after the initial row. When the piece measures approximately 7½ inches, you will be working on 292 sts and you will have completed Row 4 of the repeat. K 2 more rows and bind off. Work the remaining five side tiers in the same manner. For the foot of the bed, make three tiers, one 8 inches, one 9 inches, and one 10 inches. For the single size, cast on 104 sts. K 1 row and then work as for the tiers at the sides of the bed, this time working each tier on 156 sts. To enlarge the size to fit other beds, measure across the top only of the foot of the bed, multiply the number of inches you get by 2½, and cast on that number of sts. After working the first row, inc 1 st in every other st across the next row. Then work the necessary number of rows for each of the 8-, 9-, and 10-inch tiers.

Finishing: To complete the spread, cut a piece of fabric or existing spread large enough to span the top of the bed from side edge to side edge and from top to bottom, leaving approximately a ½-inch allowance on each side for hemming and approximately a 6-inch allowance lengthwise to allow for tucking the spread under a pillow. Hem all four edges of the piece. Then mark the piece into three sections the long way (top to bottom), having the two dividing lines one-quarter of the total width of the material in from each outside edge. Cut along these two lines. Then cut away approximately 1 inch from each cut edge. Hem each of the four cut edges with a ½-inch-deep hem. Then, using an overcast st, sew the knitted insertions in place, sewing the two strips along the four hemmed edges. Next, cut four pieces of lining material, one top piece to the size of the top portion of the spread, two side pieces to the full top-to-bottom length of the spread and as wide as the top of the bed to the floor, and one end piece to the width of the foot of the bed, again as wide as the top of the bed to the floor, allowing for ½ inch of hemming on each of these pieces. Hem each of the pieces and then sew the top lining piece in place under the top of the spread. Next, sew the three "dropped" portions in place, leaving each of the two corner portions open to accommodate bedposts if necessary. Now arrange the knitted tiers over the "dropped" lining pieces and sew them in place, overlapping the top of each by approximately ½ inch.

The Pillow

Cast on 52 sts to make the cover for the top of the pillow. K 1 row and then repeat Rows 1 through 4 of the pattern until the piece measures approximately 20 inches. K 1 more row and bind off. For the ruffled portion, cast on 195 sts and work as for the tiers on either side of the bed, working this piece on 292 sts for 6 inches. To finish the pillow, cut two pieces of lining to fit the size of the knitted piece, sew these pieces together along three sides, stuff them firmly, and then complete sewing the fourth side. For the ruffle, cut four 7-inch-wide strips of lining material, each 24 inches long, and sew them in place. Then miter and join the corners and hem the outside edge. Sew the knitted top piece to the top of the pillow. Finally, gather and fit the ruffled edging in place around the four sides, sew that in place, and seam the two short edges of the ruffle together.

A Stunning Jewel Case, Made of Pasta

Semolina #1, in various sizes and shapes and painted a perky pink, suddenly metamorphoses itself into a stunning jewel case, no one ever suspecting that the base is just an ordinary 6- by 10-inch hinged cigar box. Any size and any type of box painted in any color would do as well, and although the work involves very little effort and a minimum of materials, it is, on the whole, very rewarding. We have told in the instructions how we made our piece, but we feel that with just a little imagination on your part and a reading of our directions, you can make, if you wish, a very different and beautiful case to your own individual taste.

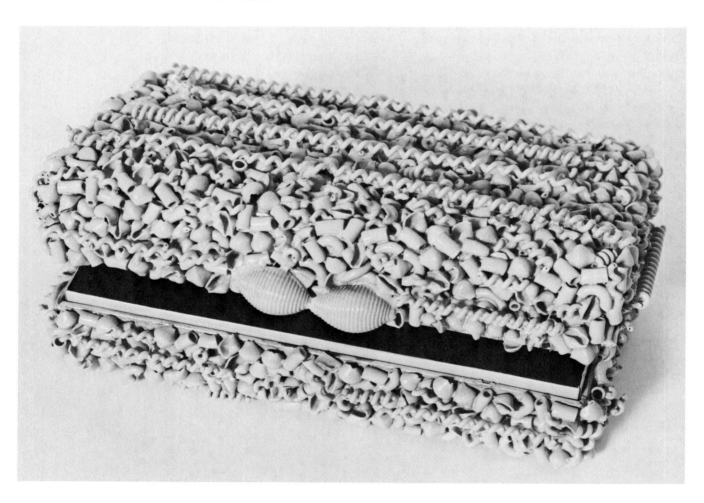

Materials:

pasta: small macaroni shells, #23; narrow fusilli, #115; ditalino, #1; the smallest-size elbow macaroni; and 2 large (approximately 1¼ inches long) macaroni shells

1 hinged cigar box, 6 × 10 inches

white glue

1 spray can enamel, in bright pink

steel crochet hook, #00 (optional)

1 ball (100 yards) Coats & Clark's "Speed-Cro-Sheen," in mid-rose (optional)

The Jewel Case

Sort the pasta by putting each variety into a separate small container or jar. Then start to work on one side of the box, finishing that side completely before starting on another. Work in the following way: Spread glue generously over a large part of the side of the box you are working on, dividing that part of the box into five or six sections at random and in different shapes as well; then quickly, while the glue is still wet, sprinkle a small handful of the ditalino over each of the glued portions. When this part of the work has been done, fit the elbows, the small shells, and broken bits of the fusilli onto those parts of the box that have not been covered on the side you are working on, fitting them in one by one as they look best, dabbing a little glue under each one and, for additional interest, turning them in different directions, with some of the shells open-side up and others open-side down. After the entire side has been covered and the pasta has set and dried into the glue, turn the box to another side and work in the same way. When the piece has been completely covered except the bottom, trim the box surfaces with long lengths of the fusilli, breaking each to the necessary length and arranging it geometrically as we did or in whatever other pattern you choose. Then glue the two large shells in position at the center front opening of the box as shown, placing them adjacent to each other and one at either side of the center. To finish the box, spray-paint the top and four sides of it. When those parts are dry, turn the box over and spray the untrimmed bottom. If desired, spray the inside of the box too. Finally, if desired, crochet a length of chain long enough to fit around the edge of the top of the box and four lengths to trim the vertical corners; glue these in place.

A Fringed Lampshade

Rows of multicolored fringe of variously textured yarns worked through the stitches of a length of plain knitting adds exciting interest to this lampshade. Our shade, for which we used four colors and three different weights of yarn, is 11 inches long and measures 6 inches in diameter across the top and 15 inches across the bottom. However, we've provided instructions for making it in any other desired size.

Materials:

2 skeins (1 ¾ ounces each) Unger Roly-Sport in color #4208 (A) and 1 skein in color #4001 (B)

1 skein (3½ ounces) Unger Roly-Poly, in color #1162 (C)

1 skein (1 4/10 ounces) Unger Fantastica, in color #204 (D)

1 pair straight knitting needles, #7

aluminum crochet hook, size C

lampshade or lampshade frame, 11 inches high × 6 inches in top diameter and 15 inches in bottom diameter

needle and thread, in pink

Gauge in Garter Stitch (knit each row): 9 stitches = 2 inches
10 rows = 1 inch

The Shade

With A, cast on 99 sts. Work even for 10 rows. Next row: *Work across 10 sts, inc 1 st in the next st, rep from * across the row (108 sts). Work even for 9 more rows. Next row: *Work across 11 sts, inc 1 st in the next st, rep from * across the row (117 sts). Work even for 9 more rows. Next row: *Work across 12 sts, inc 1 st in the next st, rep from * across the row (126 sts). Work 9 rows even. Continue now to work in this manner, increasing 9 sts evenly spaced on every tenth row and having 1 st more between each pt of inc on these rows, until there are 162 sts. Work 9 more rows even on these sts and then bind off loosely. To make a lampshade cover in a different size, work as follows: For a straight-sided shade, measure the circumference of the top, multiply this figure by the gauge to get the number of sts necessary to cast on, and then work even until the piece measures 3 inches less than the height of the shade; bind off. For example, if you are making a shade that is 10 inches high and 24 inches in circumference, you would multiply 24 inches by the 9-st-to-2-inch gauge: 24 × 9 = 216 divided by 2 = 108. Then you would cast on 108 sts and work even until the piece measures 7 inches, or 3 inches less than the full length. If you are covering a shaped shade in a different size than ours, multiply the top circumference by the gauge and cast on a number of sts equaling the nearest multiple of 9 to that figure. Then inc 9 sts evenly spaced on every tenth row until the piece measures 4 inches less than the desired length, work even for 1 inch, and bind off.

Fringing: Cut several strands of A, B, C, and D yarn, each approximately 7 inches long. Knotting two strands in every st on the right side of the cover by drawing the knots through the front lps of the sts with the crochet hook, alternate the colors across the row in the following sequence: *A, B, A, C, A, D; rep from * across. To begin the next tier, skip 5 rows of the knitted background and then knot two strands of C in every other st across. Continuing to skip 5 rows between each successive row of fringed tiers, work as follows: Third tier: Repeat the last tier, using D instead of C and placing these strands between the color-C strands of the previous row. Fourth tier: Repeat the second tier, but use color A. Fifth tier: Repeat the third tier, but use B. Sixth tier: Repeat the second tier with C. Seventh tier: Repeat the third tier with D. Eighth tier: Repeat the second tier with A. Ninth tier: Repeat the third tier with B. Tenth tier: Repeat the second tier with C. Eleventh tier: Repeat the third tier with D. Twelfth tier: Repeat the first tier.

Finishing: Fit the knitted fringed piece around the frame or shade you are using, sew the back seam, and stitch the fringed cover to the top of the frame if necessary, using an overcast stitch. Then trim evenly the ends of the bottom tier of fringe, leaving all the other tiers shaggy and untrimmed.

A Rainbow Afghan

Ten lovely shades of yarn hue into the colors of a rainbow on this beautiful knitted afghan, which measures approximately 48 by 60 inches. Worked on large needles in the ever-popular "fan and feather" stitch and accented with a natural-colored yarn, the piece will add a luxurious decorative note to any home, whether it be traditional, contemporary, or done in a period style.

Materials:
2 balls (4 ounces each) Bernat Berella "4" Knitting Worsted each in natural
    (A), lavender (B), and violet (C), and 1 ball each in coral (D), lacquer red
    (E), orange (F), old gold (G), honey (H), springleaf (I), and chartreuse (J)
1 pair straight knitting needles, #11
tapestry needle, #18

Pattern Stitch: *Rows 1 and 4:* K. *Row 2:* P. *Row 3:* (K 2 tog) three times, *(yo,
k 1) six times, (k 2 tog) six times, rep from * across the row, and end (k 2 tog)
three times. Repeat these 4 rows for the pattern stitch.

Gauge in Pattern Stitch: 9 stitches = 2 inches

The Afghan

Make three pieces: With A, cast on 72 sts. Work even in pat st and, working 4
rows in each color, follow the color sequence of *A, B, C, D, E, F, G, H, I, J, C,
B, A, B, C, J, I, H, G, F, E, D, C, B. Rep from * twice and end with 4 rows of A.
Bind off.

   Finishing: Sew the strips together, matching the stripes and sewing with
color over color.

Irish Knit Pillows

This pair of big, 21-inch-square pillows, coordinated in design and made to be used either separately or together, are knitted on large needles to a loose gauge. Made of real fisherman yarn, both are richly textured with traditional cables and popcorns, although one is a little more full in design than the other for the sake of contrast.

 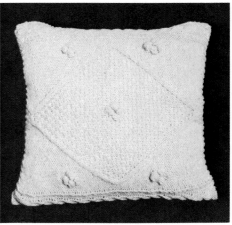

Materials:

3 skeins (2 ounces each) Bernat Blarney-Spun for each pillow
1 pair straight knitting needles, #10
1 double-pointed needle, #10
¾ yard natural linen, 45 inches wide, for each pillow
1½ pounds polyester stuffing material for each pillow
needle and thread, in natural

Gauge: 7 stitches = 2 inches

The Fancier Pillow

Cast on 67 sts. Row 1 (wrong side): *K 1 through the back lp of the st, p 1, rep from * across the row, and end with a k 1 through the back lp of the last st. Row 2 (right side): *P 1, k 1 through the back lp of the next st, rep from * across the row, and end with p 1. Rep these 2 rows twice more for the ribbed border. Starting on the wrong side now, work the first row of the pattern as follows: *K 1, p 1, k 2, p 2, p the next st and inc 1 in that st, k 2, p 1, k 2, p 3, p the next st and inc in that st, p 3, k 2, p 1, k 9, p 2*, p 1 for the center st. Then rep between *'s once, following the pattern in reverse (working from the last st to the first). There are now 71 sts on the needle and the pattern is set. To complete the pattern, follow Chart A. All even rows are marked on the chart but odd rows are not because all the sts on these rows are worked as they appear on this side of the work: Those sts that have been purled on the previous row will appear as k sts and should be knitted and those that have been knitted will appear as p sts and should be purled. Note that on the first pattern repeat, rows 2

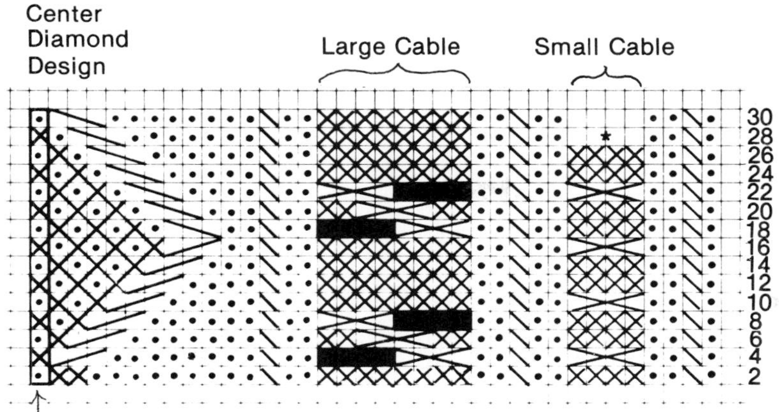

Center Diamond Design

Large Cable   Small Cable

Chart A

* return to row 4

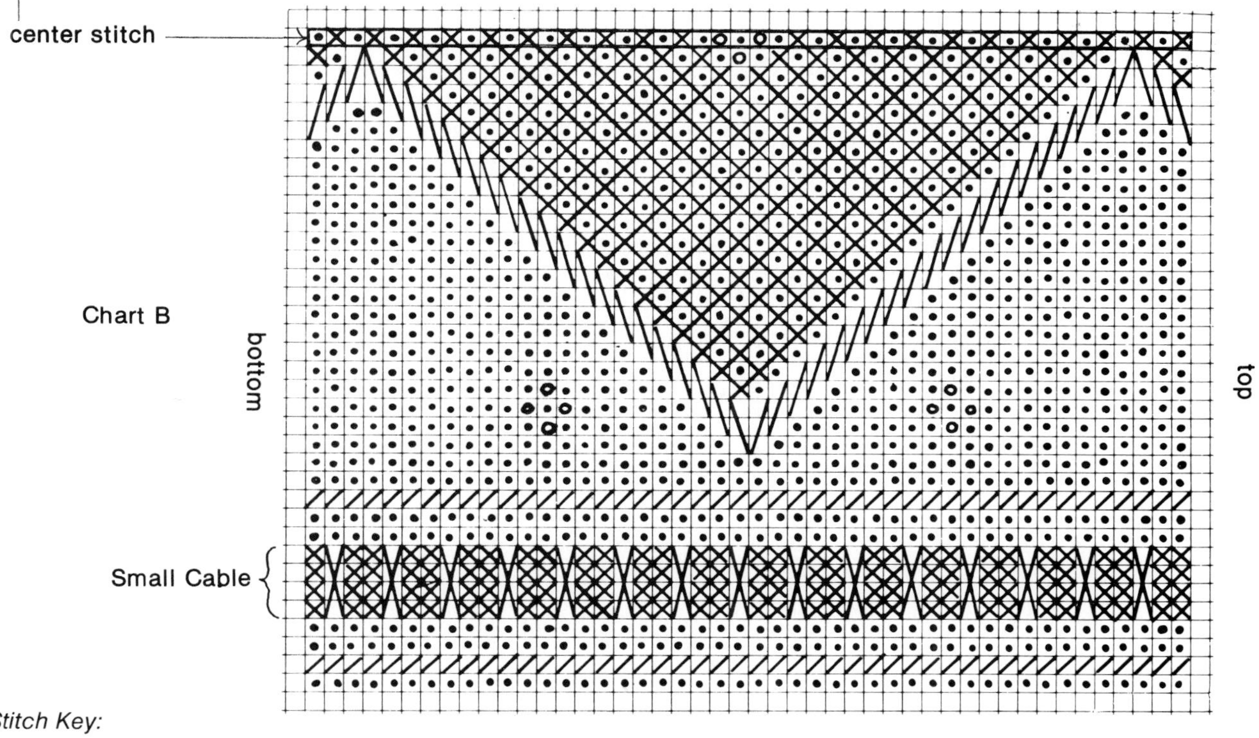

center stitch

Chart B

bottom

top

Small Cable

Stitch Key:

× = k

• = p

\ = twisted k st (k through back lp of st)

✕ = sl 2 sts on the dp needle and hold in front of work, k the next 2 sts, and k the sts from the dp needle

▬ = sl the next 2 sts on the dp needle, hold these sts at the back of the work, k the next 2 sts, then k the 2 sts from the dp needle

╱ = sl 1 st on the dp needle and leave at back of work, k the next 2 sts, then p the st from the dp needle

╲ = sl 2 sts on the dp needle and leave at front of work, p the next st, then k 2 sts from the dp needle

○ = popcorn stitch: Sl the st to be worked onto the right needle, turn the work to the wrong side, k into the back lp of the slipped st, then p into the front lp of the same st, k into the back lp, and p into the front lp. Turn the work to the right side now and k each of these 4 sts, turn again, and p each of the sts. Turn the piece once more to the right side and slip the second, third, and fourth sts over the first. Place the popcorn st on the right needle and continue across the row.

89

through 31 are worked as shown on the chart except for the small cable. Here the pattern repeat returns to Row 4 after the 27th row has been completed. That sequence is then repeated through Row 21 and the completion of the knitting of the pillow. Note also that the center diamond design and the large cable at either side of it are repeated twice more and that the pattern ends with Rows 4 through 9 of these designs. Third, note that all sts are worked to within 1 st of the center st and from then on—from 1 st after the center st—they are worked in reverse, which means that the outline of the center diamond and the other cables are worked from that point with a reverse twist. For example, when the cable twist on the first half of the chart reads "sl 2 sts on the dp needle and hold in front of work, then k the next 2 sts, and k the sts from the dp needle," the repeat should be worked as follows: "sl the next 2 sts on the dp needle, hold these sts at the back of the work, k the next 2 sts, then k the 2 sts from the dp needle." When the entire pattern has been worked, dec 4 sts on the last row, just as you increased on the first row of the pattern. Then finish the knitted portion of the pillow with 5 rows of ribbing made as at the start and make a bind-off row in the ribbing as established.

Finishing: Cut two pieces of the linen, each 21½ inches square. Seam these pieces together on three sides, stuff them firmly (making special note to fill in the four corners), sew the fourth side, stretch the knitted piece over one side, and stitch it in place with an overcast stitch. Finally, cut four lengths of yarn, each approximately 12 inches long, and wrap one strand around each stuffed corner of the pillow, wrapping the yarn tightly to shape each corner. Tie the yarn securely in place and cut off the ends.

The More Simple Pillow

Start as for the fancier pillow, working the ribbing in the same manner. Then, starting on the wrong side, work the first row of the pattern as follows: *K 1, p 1, k 2, p 2 , inc 1 in the next st as if to p, k 2, p 1, k 5, inc in the next st as if to k, k 12, p 2, k 2, p 1 *, k 1 for the center st. Then rep between *'s once, following the pattern in reverse in the same manner as established on the first row of the pattern for the Fancier Pillow. To complete the pattern, follow Chart B, working all even rows as marked and all odd rows as they were worked on Chart A and reversing the pattern after the center st, as on Chart A.

Finishing: Assemble, line, stuff, and finish this pillow as the first, eliminating the twisting and tying of the four corners.

Director's Chair Seat and Back Insets

Latchet-hooked and contemporary in design, the insets shown here are soft and luxurious and fitting for the most comfortable chair in the house. Worked in russet and black, our design is shown on a wood-framed chair, although the pieces can be worked for any director's chair that is made for removable insets. Our pieces are made to fit a standard-size director's chair with a 15- by 19-inch seat and a 7- by 24-inch back. Included in the instructions are directions for extending the design to whatever dimensions are necessary for your own particular chair. The pattern may, of course, be worked in your own choice of colors.

Materials:

1 piece rug canvas, 4 spaces to 1 inch, 26 inches square
masking tape
10 skeins (70 yards each) Columbia-Minerva Great Ideas in russet and 6 skeins in black
latchet hook
needle and carpet thread, in black
¾ yard medium-weight canvas, 36 inches wide, in russet (for lining)
aluminum crochet hook, size H
2 dowel rods, 1 inch in diameter, each 15 inches long

The Insets

Seat: Cut a piece of rug canvas to measure 17 by 20 inches and bind the edges

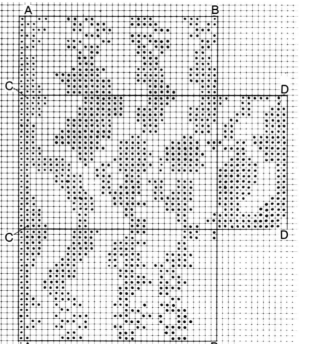

Seat: Work pattern from B to A, work center row, and then work pattern from A to B to the left of the center row.

Back: Work pattern from D to C, work center row, and then work pattern from C to D to the left of the center row.

Center Row —⌐

Color Key:
□ = russet
• = black

with the masking tape. Cut a portion of the yarn into 5-inch strands and, following the chart for the design, work the pattern to completion with the latchet hook. To finish this part of the chair cover, remove the masking tape, fold under 2 of the unworked rows on each of the four sides of the piece, cut away the remaining unworked canvas, and tack the folded-under edges into place. Cut a piece of canvas lining material to measure ½ inch larger than the seat in the width and 2½ inches longer. Turn under a ¼-inch-wide hem along each of the two long edges and sew the hems in place; repeat along the two short edges and then fold 1 inch of each of these short edges around one of the dowel sticks. Finally, sew, wrong sides together, the hemmed piece of lining to the latchet-hooked piece of work, allowing the dowel-covered portion at each short end to extend beyond the hemmed piece so that the piece can be more easily inserted into the chair frame. (For chair seats that are longer or wider than the size for which this seat has been designed, follow the same procedure as above but start with as much extra rug canvas and lining material as necessary and continue to work the latchet-hooked pattern as established until the rug canvas piece is filled).

Back: Cut a piece, of rug canvas to measure 9 by 26 inches, bind the edges, and then latch-hook the design as indicated on the chart. To finish the piece, cut and hem the canvas edges as for the seat of the chair. Then, with the russet yarn, crochet a tab at each short edge to fit around the extended spoke at each side of the top of the back of the chair frame. Work these pieces on 24 sts each, working the first row on each side directly into the canvas and then working 5 more rows of single crochet in the usual way. Finally, cut the lining material to fit the piece, allowing ¼ inch extra for hemming on each of the four sides and extending the lining on each short edge only to the point where the crocheted tabs begin (these tabs are not to be lined). Hem and sew the lining in place. Then fold over the extended crocheted portions and sew the long edges to the lining, leaving the top and bottom of the tabs open to allow for the insertion of this piece onto the back of the chair.

FUN FOR KITCHENS

An Arrangement for Rooting Plants

Vino for "wine," or the bottles that once contained wine, and *vida* for "life"—painted words on an enameled board—create the perfect setting for rooting plants to take life. Three emptied green-glass wine bottles, the same in shape and perhaps a little different in size—or, actually, any size or shape you want—filled with fresh water provide the rooting medium. Hung from varying lengths of colored macramé cords attached to three cup hooks at the bottom of the board, this attractive composition adds an unusual touch to a kitchen or dining room window.

Materials:
1 piece plywood, 1 inch thick, 3¼ × 16 inches
3 cup hooks
2 screw eyes
1 spray can enamel, in white
tracing paper
carbon paper
masking tape
Testor's Model Paint in leaf green (A), insignia red (B), and lemon yellow (C)
artist's fine paintbrush
3 balls (4 ounces each) Bernat Big Berella Bulky, in hunter green
aluminum crochet hook, size K
3 oval or round-bottomed wine bottles, approximately 7½ inches high
small amount of strong, thin wire
needle and thread, in green

The Planter

Spray the plywood, the cup hooks, and the screw eyes with the white paint. Then trace the letters for *Vino Vida* from the alphabet chart on page 160 on the tracing paper. Tape a sheet of carbon paper, face down, over the board and draw around the letters on the tracing paper, making sure to space the letters evenly and to align them across the center of the width of the board. In the same manner, trace and transfer the decorative portions onto the board, ar-

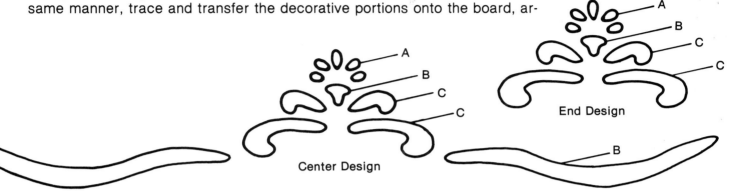

Center Design

End Design

ranging them as shown in the photograph. Paint the designs, following the colors indicated. Make the macramé cords for the arrangement in the following way: Cut two strands of yarn 100 inches long and two 180 inches; these four strands will make the shortest cord of the arrangement, measuring approximately 9½ inches when finished. Next, cut two strands 150 inches long and two 220 inches; these will become the medium-length cord, measuring approximately 14½ inches when finished. Finally, cut two 200 inches long and two 320 inches for the longest cord, which will measure approximately 20½ inches when done. Using the two shorter cords as the foundation cords and the two longer ones as the working cords, start the shortest cord by folding the four strands cut for it in half and tying a slipknot 1 inch below the center fold. This establishes the hanging loop at the top of the cord. Then work *25 half square knots, slide them upward tightly to form a 3½-inch spiral, leave 1½ inches unworked, and make a square knot. Repeat from * once, separating the unworked 1½ inches at the end of the repeat to make two square knots—using two cords only for each—at the bottom. Cut off the remaining lengths of cord. Work the two other cords in the same manner, repeating from * twice for the 14½-inch cord and three times for the 20½-inch cord.

Finishing: With triple strands of yarn, crochet three chains to fit around the necks of the three bottles you are using, crocheting them over wire cut to measure approximately 1½ inches longer than the diameters of the necks. Twist the ends of the crochet-covered wires very tightly around the bottle necks and securely sew the two bottom square knots to the chain, one at either side of the neck. Finally, screw the cup hooks into the bottom edge of the board, placing one in the center and each of the remaining two 2 inches in from each end. Insert each of the two screw eyes on the top edge of the board above the two side cup hooks. Cut four strands of yarn to the desired length for the hanging of your arrangement and, placing them together, knot the ends through each screw eye. Hang the bottles over the cup hooks with the longest one in the center, or in any other desired manner.

Color Key:
A = leaf green
B = lemon yellow
C = insignia red

A Trio of Hanging Skillets

Attractively painted with illustrations of foods and further embellished with colorful single-crochet chains, these hanging skillets will add a graphic touch to any kitchen wall.

Materials:

3 skillets, each 8½ inches in bottom diameter, with holes in the handles for hanging

1 spray can enamel, in white

tracing paper

masking tape

carbon paper

artist's fine paintbrush

Testor's Model Paint in insignia red (A), leaf green (B), pea green (C), insignia orange (D), lemon yellow (E), and flat roof brown (F), the last to be mixed with insignia red to make the purple

felt-tipped marking pen, in black

aluminum crochet hook, size E

small amounts of sport yarn in bright shades of red (A), orange (B), yellow (C), and green (D)

rubber cement

The Skillets

Thoroughly spray each skillet with the white enamel and allow it to dry. Then trace the patterns on tracing paper. Next, with the masking tape, tape a sheet of carbon, face down over the bottom of one skillet, lay Design 1 on top, and

Design 1

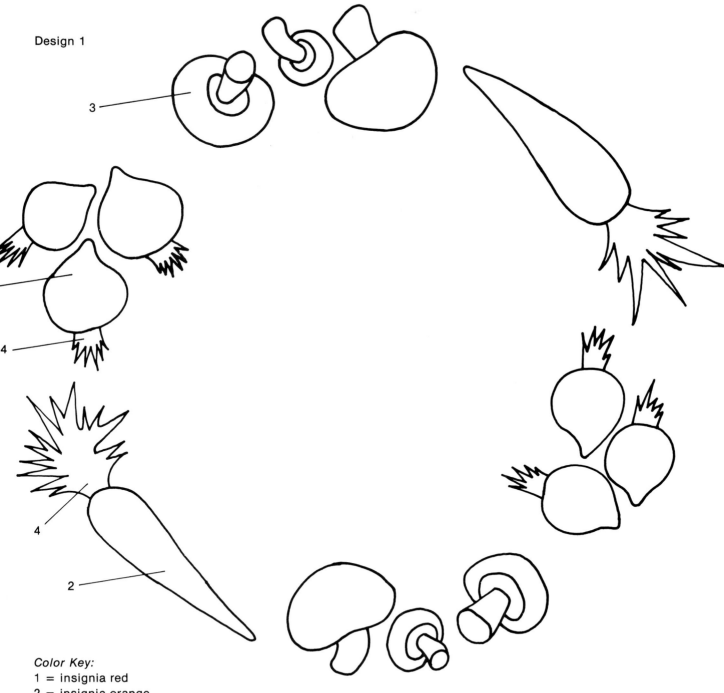

Color Key:
1 = insignia red
2 = insignia orange
3 = lemon yellow
4 = leaf green

All outlining done in black

97

Design 2

Color Key:
1 = insignia red
2 = purple
3 = insignia orange
4 = lemon yellow
5 = pea green
6 = leaf green
7 = black
All outlining done in black

6

4

4

5

6

6

2

1

6

6

3

6

98

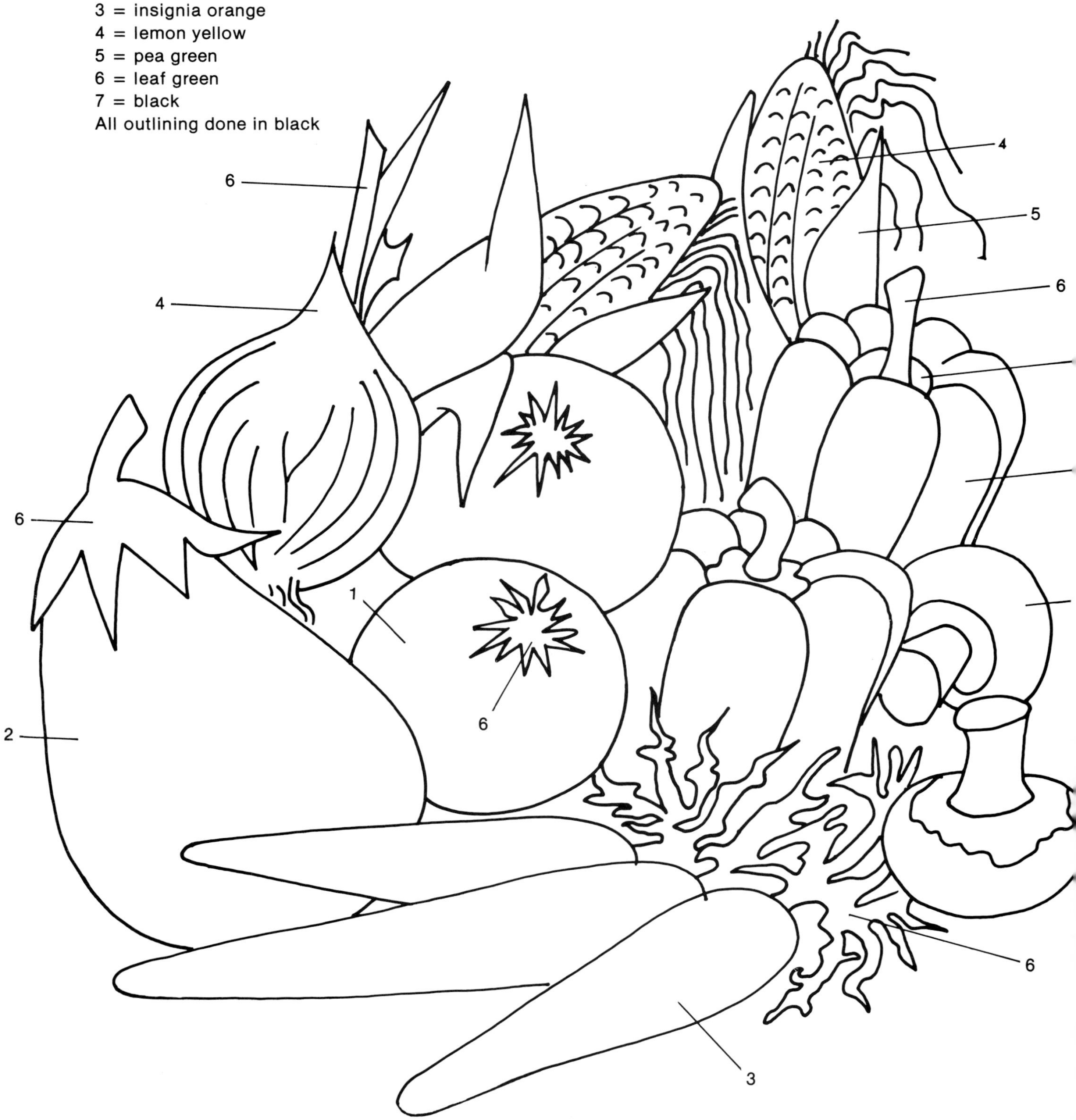

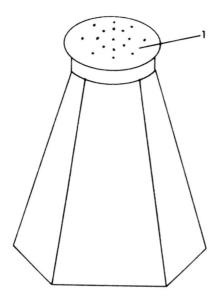

outline it on the painted surface; repeat with a second skillet. Then lay Design 2 over carbon on the third skillet and trace it. Paint the designs according to the color key. When dry, outline each item with the black marking pen. To finish the skillet designs, transfer one shaker pattern onto the center of the two skillets painted with Design 1, outlining the shakers with the marking pen and filling in the caps. Finally, draw freehand with the black pen an "S" for salt on one of the shakers and a "P" for pepper on the other.

Finishing: Crochet four chains of 240 sts each in colors A, B, C, and D. Trim the side edges of each pan as follows: Measure and mark eight equal points around the lip of each skillet. Then arrange each of the four chains, in order of A, B, C, and D, into scallops, beginning a new scallop at each mark. Cement the chains in place at the marks. To make the hanging loop for each pan, ch 40 with double strands of A. Join the ends with a sl st to form a ring. Place the ring through the opening in the handle of the skillet and slipknot it in place.

A Set of Gay Cannisters

Ordinary cannisters made gay with bright Contact-paper covers are identified by white vinyl labels reembroidered with letters of the alphabet. Ours are covered with a red-and-white-checked gingham, although yours can be made coordinated to the colors of your own kitchen, even, perhaps, covered with small pieces of wallpaper left over from the last time the walls were done. And, of course, the shape of the cannisters can be round or square.

Materials:

1 yard Contact paper, 14 inches wide, in any desired color
4 cannisters, the largest one 5½ inches high (without the cover) and 19½ inches in diameter at its widest point
¼ yard vinyl, in contrasting color to Contact paper
tracing paper
carbon paper
1 ball (175 yards) Coats & Clark's "Knit-Cro-Sheen," in black
sharp-pointed embroidery needle
rubber cement
3½ yards narrow cord, in black or color to contrast with vinyl

The Cannisters

Cut one piece of Contact paper to fit around each cannister and adhere each to its cannister, overlapping the edges at what will become the back and making sure that the pattern edges meet. Miter the bottom edges if necessary. Now make an identifying label for each by cutting a piece of vinyl long enough to fit diagonally from the top to the bottom of the front of each cannister. Shape the short edges to a point. Trace the desired letters from the alphabet chart on page 160 on tracing paper. Then tape a sheet of carbon face down over each piece of vinyl and outline the necessary letters on each one, spacing them evenly. Using satin stitch, embroider over the traced letters with single strands of the "Knit-Cro-Sheen". Cement the embroidered labels in place on the front of each cannister. Trim the edges of the labels and the top of each cannister, just below the covering lid, with the black cord, cutting it to fit and cementing it in place.

A Decorative Hanging Tray Holder

Functional, convenient, and a splashy graphic note for any kitchen wall with its colorful variety of tiny crocheted fruits and vegetables appliqued onto a gros-pointed background, our tray holder is made to keep anywhere from one to four trays of different sizes at your fingertips. The piece, which hangs from a 5-inch metal ring, is finished with a grosgrain ribbon lining.

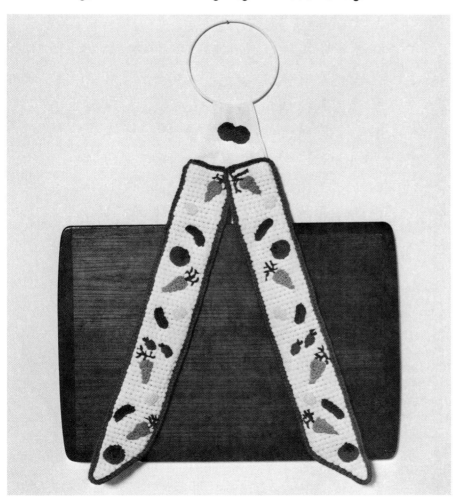

Materials:
2 strips rug canvas, 4 spaces to 1 inch, each 4 × 20 inches
masking tape
1 ball (4 ounces) Bernat Big Berella Bulky, in white (MC)
tapestry needle, #18
needle and thread, in white
aluminum crochet hook, size D
1 ball (2 ounces) Bernat Berella Sportspun in scarlet (A),
     1 ball in orange (B), 1 ball in yellow (C), and 1 ball in shannon green (D)
3 yards grosgrain ribbon, 2½ inches wide, in white
metal ring, 5 inches in diameter, in white

Leaves are worked in outline stitch

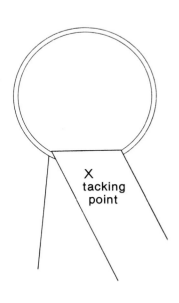

X
tacking
point

Gauge in Single Crochet: 6 stitches = 1 inch

The Tray Holder

Grospointed strips (Make two): Bind the edges of each strip of rug canvas with masking tape. Then with MC and the Kalem stitch, embroider horizontally across 9 spaces for 15½ inches. Then shape the piece to a point by embroidering 1 st less at one side edge on every row until 1 st remains, reversing the side on which the decrease is made on each of the two pieces. Finish each of these pieces by cutting away all excess canvas except for 2 rows along each edge. Turn the 2 rows under and hem them in place. Then with MC, work 1 row of sc around, working directly through the last embroidered canvas space and working 3 sc in each corner st as you turn; fasten off. With A, work 1 more rnd of sc.

Crocheted Fruits and Vegetables

Carrots (Make eight): With B, ch 5 and then work even on 4 sc for 2 rows. Next 2 rows: (Sk 1 sc, sc in the next sc) twice (2 sts remain). Work in sc on these 2 sts for 2 rows. On the next row, sk 1 sc, sc in the one remaining sc, ch 1, and turn. Work once more into the 1 sc and then fasten off.

Tomatoes (Make six): With A, ch 2 and then work 5 sc in the second ch from hook. Next rnd: Work 2 sc in each sc around (10 sc). Next rnd: *1 sc in the first st, 2 sc in the next, rep from * around (15 sc). End the rnd with a sl st in the first sc of the previous rnd and fasten off.

Radishes (Make four): With A, ch 2 and then work 1 sc in the second ch from hook, ch 1, and turn. Next row: Work 3 sc in the 1 sc of the previous row. Next row: Work 3 sc tog and fasten off.

Lemons (Make six): With C, ch 2 and turn. Work 3 sc in the second ch from hook, ch 1, and turn. Work 1 row even on 3 sc, ch 1, and turn. On the next row, work 3 sc tog and fasten off.

Cucumbers (Make six): With D, ch 9 and then work in sc on 8 sts for 1 row. Working around now, work 1 sl st in each st and fasten off along the opposite side of the chain.

Finishing: Arrange the crocheted pieces on the strips as shown in the photograph or as desired, positioning four carrots, three lemons, three cucumbers, two tomatoes, and two radishes on each strip. Sew them in place. Then with D and an outline stitch, embroider stems and leaves on the carrots, tomatoes, and radishes, as shown in the illustration. To complete the piece, cut the ribbon into two 46-inch-long strips. Holding the two pieces together, cut the ends at diagonals so that they match the diagonals at the ends of the embroidered strips. The points on two of these will be facing in one direction and the other two in the other. Seam the matching diagonals together and turn the piece right side out. Thread the joined piece through the metal ring so that the points face outward and draw the ends to an even length. Spread the portion of the ribbons crossing the ring slightly apart, as shown in the illustration, and tack them in place approximately 1 inch below the ring. Sew the two remaining tomatoes over the tacking and embroider stems on them as on the other tomatoes. Then sew the grospointed pieces to the top layer of each of the ribbons, leaving the bottom layers free. Insert your trays through the two layers of ribbon.

102

The Market Bag

Looking really real but actually just a gay conversation piece designed to hang on your kitchen wall, our market bag is crocheted with white mercerized cotton in the attractive knot stitch and it's chockful of colorful crocheted fruits and vegetables and real bread and rolls, this last group forever preserved with layers of clear varnish.

Materials:
2 balls (100 yards each) Coats & Clark's "Speed-Cro-Sheen," in white (MC)
1 skein (2 ounces) Coats & Clark's Red Heart Sport Yarn in red (A), 1 skein in
    paddy green (B), 1 skein in daffodil (C), and 1 skein in vibrant orange (D)
aluminum crochet hook, size G
needle and thread, in green
1 loaf of Italian bread, one loaf of pumpernickel, and six round hard rolls
1 spray can clear varnish
stuffing material
tapestry needle, #18

Pattern Stitch: *Row 1:* *Draw up lp on hook to ½ inch, yo and draw through, insert hook between long lp and single strand, yo and draw through, yo and draw through 2 lps on hook (single knot st made), 1 single knot st (double knot st made), sk 4 ch, 1 sc in next ch, rep from * across and end 1 sc in last ch, 1 double knot st, 1 single knot st, turn. Row 2: Sk first single knot st, *1 sc between long lp and single strand of the first half of next double knot st, 1 sc between long lp and single strand of second half of same double knot st, 1 double knot st, rep from * across and end 1 double knot st, 1 single knot st, turn. *Row 3:* Skip first single knot st, *1 sc between long lp and single strand of first half of next double knot st, 1 sc between long lp and single strand of second half of same double knot st, 1 double knot st, rep from * across and end 1 sc in turning knot st of previous row, 1 double knot st, 1 single knot st, turn. Repeat Row 3 for pattern.

Gauge in Single Crochet: 9 stitches = 2 inches

The Market Bag

With MC, ch 120. Work even in pat st for 20 inches, ch 1, and turn at the end of the last row. Next row: *Sc in the first lp, sc in the knot st, sc in the second lp, 2 sc in the next sc, rep from * across, ch 1, and turn. Next row: Work 1 sc in each sc across, ch 1, and turn. *Casing:* Sc in the first sc, *ch 1, sk 1 sc, sc in the next sc, rep from * and end with 1 sc in the last sc, ch 1, and turn. Next row: Work 1 sc in each sc and in each ch-1 sp across. Fasten off. To finish the bag, fold it in half widthwise, with wrong sides together. To join one side and the bottom, work as follows across one short and one long edge: Work a sc with a ch-1 between along these two open edges (the third, short open edge will become the top of the bag), working the sts into the lps and the sc "knots" and adding enough sts so that the work lies flat. Continuing around, work in the same manner across the opposite side of the bag, working through the double thicknesses of the bag on this side. Ch 1 and turn at the end of the rnd. Then work 1 sc in each sc and in each ch-1 sp around, ch 1, and turn. Next rnd: Work 1 sc in each sc around the three sides. Fasten off. To complete the bag itself, make a drawstring as follows: With double strands of MC, ch 110 and fasten off. Weave the drawstring through the openings of the casing and knot the ends together.

The Fruits and Vegetables

Tomatoes (Make one small and one large one): With A, ch 2 and then work 6 sc in the second ch from hook. Next rnd: Work 2 sc in each st around (12 sc). Next rnd: *1 sc in the first sc, 2 sc in the next sc, rep from * around (18 sc). Next rnd: *1 sc in each of the first 2 sc, 2 sc in the next sc, rep from * around (24 sc). Continuing in this manner, increase 6 sts evenly spaced on every rnd until there are 60 sts in all. Then work even in sc on 60 sts for 6 rnds for the small tomato and 10 rnds for the large one. To finish both tomatoes, continue working around, decreasing 1 st in every other st until all sts are gone and stuffing the pieces firmly as you close them. When all sts are gone and the pieces are firmly stuffed, join the last rnd with a sl st to the first st and fasten off. To make a stem for the small tomato, *ch 5 with B and turn. Sl st in each of the first 4

▲ *A Bright Covering for Your Barbecue Grill, p. 136; The Barbecue Butler, p. 130; A Decorative Shield for Outdoor Hors d'Oeuvres, p. 134; A Set of Bright Placemats, Designed for Outdoor Dining, p. 138.*

◄ *A Decorative Hanging Tray Holder, p. 101; Knitted Numbered Stair Treads, p. 39; A Trio of Hanging Skillets, p. 96; The Market Bag, p. 103.*

sts, rep from * four times, and then join the last to the first ch and fasten off, leaving a short length of yarn. Finally, draw the remaining strand through the inner ring of the piece, forming a stem. Sew the stem to the top of the tomato. To make the large stem, *ch 7 and turn. Sl st in each of the first 6 sts, rep from * four times more, and finish as for the small stem. To give the tomatoes their characteristic shape, work 5 giant overcast stitches with double strands of A, working through the pieces from center top to center bottom and then back up again to the center top on the opposite side.

Carrots (Make one small and two large ones): With D, work as for the tomatoes, increasing 6 sts evenly spaced until there are 24 sts in all for the small carrot and 30 for the large ones. Work even for 5 rnds for the small one and 8 for the large. On the next rnd, dec 6 sts evenly spaced (18 sts for the small one and 24 for the large). Work even now on the 18 sts for 1 inch and on the 24 for 1½ inches. For the small one, dec 6 sts evenly spaced on the next rnd (12 sts) and then work 2 sts tog on following rnds until all sts are gone, stuffing the piece as you go. On the 24 sts, work even for 1½ inches more and then dec 6 sts evenly spaced on the next rnd (18 sts). Finish the bottom in the same manner as the small one was finished. Make three stems as follows: With B, ch 13. Sc on 12 sts for 2 rows, *ch 12, turn, sl st in each of the next 5 ch, ch 6, turn, sl st in each of the next 5 ch, then sl st in the remaining unworked 6 ch of the ch-12, rep from * once, join with a sl st to the first st of the first sc row, and fasten off. Fold the starting 2 sc rows in half lengthwise and sew the edges together with an overcast st. Sew the stems to the carrot tops. To complete each carrot, attach double strands of D to the top (the stem portion) and wrap them around the carrot diagonally, working toward the bottom tip. Break off the yarn and attach the end to the tip.

Cucumber: With B, ch 2 and then work as for the tomatoes until there are 24 sts. Work 2 rnds even on 24 sts. Then on the next rnd, inc 6 sts evenly spaced (30 sts). Work 2 rnds even on 30 sts, and then inc to 36 sts. Work 24 rnds even on 36 sts. Dec 6 sts evenly spaced now on every third rnd until 6 sts remain, stuffing the piece firmly as you work. Break off yarn, leaving a long thread. Draw the thread tightly through the remaining 6 sts and fasten off. To add texture to the piece, embroider French knots with double strands of B at random over the surface.

Lemons (Make two): With C, work as for the tomatoes, increasing 6 sts evenly spaced on every other rnd until there are 30 sts. Work even on 30 sts for 9 rnds. Then dec 6 sts on every other rnd until 6 sts remain, stuffing the piece firmly as you decrease. Work 1 rnd even on the remaining 6 sts. Then break off yarn, leaving a long thread, draw the thread tightly through the remaining 6 sts, and fasten off.

Finishing: Spray the bread and rolls with three coats of varnish, allowing drying time after each coat. Finally, put all the pieces into the bag, arranging them so that colors are evenly distributed, a portion of the Italian loaf extends out of the top of the bag, and one small and one large carrot hang over onto the outside of the bag, as shown in the photograph. With MC, firmly tack each of the fruits and vegetables in place so that the weight of the breadstuff does not dislodge them. Also, tack the front crocheted portion of the bag to the back, just below those breadstuffs that need to be kept from slipping to the bottom of the bag.

AND FOR THE BATHROOM

Macramed Fishnet

Slipknots, half square knots, and a few balls of mercerized crochet cotton are worked together here to make a most unusual 6- by 8-foot wall hanging to drape over a bathroom, bedroom, or den wall or ceiling, or even over an outdoor terrace wall. The piece becomes especially effective—and suitable for a beach house—when it is trimmed with some small seashells, bits of cork, a starfish or two, a seahorse, and other ocean-bottom fossils, such as branches of coral.

Materials:

4 balls (100 yards each) Coats & Clark's "Speed-Cro-Sheen," in eggshell
1 piece medium-weight cardboard or Styrofoam, approximately
    24 inches square
sea "findings"

The Net

Cut a length of the thread to 8½ feet for the foundation cord, forty-eight strands each to 12 feet for the working cords, and sixty-four strands each to 9 feet. Attach each of the sixty-four short strands to the foundation cord, attaching each one with a slipknot and spacing them 1½ inches apart. Pin 2 feet of this "strung" foundation cord to the cardboard or Styrofoam working surface, securing each of the slipknots with a straight pin and leaving the balance of the cord hanging free to one side to be worked later. Start to macramé as follows: For the first row, attach one of the 12-foot strands to the first of the hanging 9-foot strands with a square knot 1½ inches below the foundation cord; pin the knot in place on the working surface. Then carry the same 12-foot strand to the next 9-foot strand, make another square knot with these two strands, and pin it in place. Continue working in this way across the width of the 2-foot working surface. Now drop the remainder of the 12-foot working cord and attach another 12-foot cord to the first 9-foot cord at the beginning of the row, 1½ inches below the first row of knots. Work a second row of knots in the same manner as the first row, again pinning each knot in place to ensure proper spacing. When you have reached the end of the working surface with this row, continue with a third and fourth row and as many subsequent rows as are necessary to cover the length of the 2-foot working surface. Now remove all pins, slip the knotted piece upward off the top of the board, pin the last knotted row at the top for a new starting row, and continue working as before for another 2 feet. Repeat this process once more. At this point, you should have a piece measuring 2 feet wide by 6 feet long. Drop this piece off the left side of the working board, shift 2 more feet of the foundation cord onto the board, pin it in place at the top, and continue working square knots over this piece as on the first piece. When this portion of the net has been done, work a third and a fourth section in the same way. When completed, the piece should measure 8 feet wide by 6 feet long.

Finishing: Trim all remaining loose threads to approximately ½ inch below and at either side of the last rows of knots. Then drape the piece as shown, or as desired, over nails or with wood staples. Sew or glue whatever sea "findings" you have chosen to use onto the net in whatever arrangement you wish.

A Hairpin-Lace Shower Curtain

Delicate bands of hairpin lace form the charming undulating-wave pattern of this shower curtain. Hung over a white plastic liner, it is worked in cool shades of the sea in a four-ply machine-washable-and-dryable yarn.

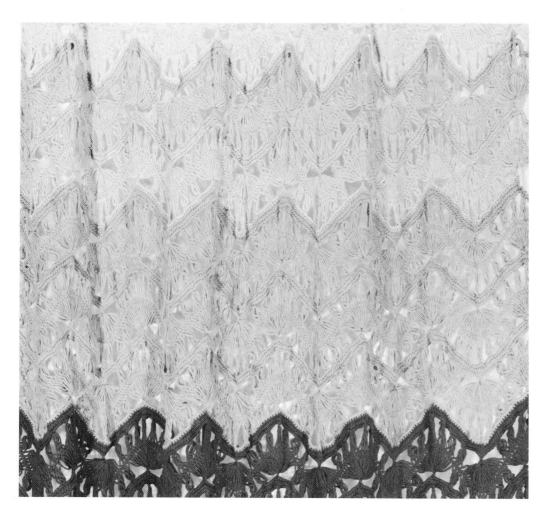

Materials:

4 skeins (4 ounces each) Columbia-Minerva 100% Orlon Acrylic Nantuk 4-ply
    in dark turquoise (A), 3 skeins in turquoise (B), 2 skeins in bright turquoise
    (C), and 1 skein in baby green (D)
adjustable hairpin-lace loom
aluminum crochet hook, size K
wool needle
needle and thread, in white and turquoise shades
plastic shower-curtain liner with holes for 10 rings, in white
10 metal washers, each ¾ inch in diameter
10 plastic snap-on shower-curtain rings

Gauge in Single Crochet: 3 stitches = 1 inch

The Shower Curtain

Hairpin-lace strips: With the loom adjusted to 4 inches, make ten strips, four in A, three in B, two in C, and one in D, each having 315 lps on each side of the loom. Finish each of the strips with color over color in the following way: For the upper edge on each strip: *(Sc 3 lps tog, ch 5) 7 times, sc 21 lps tog, rep from * across the row, and end with (sc 3 lps tog, ch 5) 7 times. Ch 1 more to turn; then work 1 sc in each of the first 5 ch, 1 sc in each sc, and 5 sc in each ch-5 lp across the row. Fasten off. For the lower edge: *Sc 21 lps tog, ch 5, (sc 3 lps tog, ch 5) 7 times, rep from * across, and end with sc 21 lps tog, ch 1, and turn. Complete this edge by working 1 sc in each sc and 5 sc in each ch-5 lp across; then fasten off. Join the four A strips for the bottom of the curtain by sewing them together with an overcast stitch and yarn in the same color. Then join the next three B strips to each other in the same way and then the next two C. Arrange the strips in a color sequence ranging from A at the bottom to D at the top. Work 1 more row of sc along the top edge of each of the A, B, and C sections, in each case working this row in the color of the next strip to which it is to be joined. Finally sew these strips together, again using yarn in color over color.

Finishing: Bottom edge: Ch 17 with A. Then with the right side of the work facing, join to the first sc on the bottom row, work 1 sc in that st and in each of the next 41 sts, sc 3 sts tog, *sc in each of the next 40 sts, sc 3 sts tog, rep from * four times more, sc in each of the next 42 sts, ch 18, and turn. Next row: Sc in the second ch from hook and in each of the next 16 ch, *sc in each sc across the row to 1 st before the dec on the previous row, sc the next 3 sts tog, rep from * across, and end the row by working 1 sc in each of the next 17 ch, ch 1, and turn. Next row: Sk 1 st (dec), rep the last row to within the last 2 sts, sk 1 st (dec), sc in the last st, ch 1, and turn. Rep the last row twice more and fasten off. Top edge: With D and the right side of work facing, attach yarn to the corner st, *work 1 sc in each of the first 40 sc, sc 3 tog, rep from * 6 times more, work 1 sc in each of the last 42 sc, ch 1, and turn. Work 4 more rows of sc as on the bottom row, decreasing 1 st at beginning and end of each row and working 3 sc tog over each group of the 3 sc tog on the previous row. Side edges: Starting at the lower edge with A and with the right side of work facing, attach yarn to the corner st. Working from A to D, work 5 sc along the bottom edge, *ch 12, work 1 sc in each of the first 4 free sc of the next scallop, rep from * 3 times, change to B, rep from * three times more. Then with C, rep from * twice. With D, ch 12, work 6 sc along the top border, ch 7 for a tab, and turn. Work 1 more row of sc along this edge, working color over color and working 1 sc in each sc and in each ch st of the previous row. Fasten off. Work the other side edge to correspond, starting at the top by chaining 6 for a tab and then reversing the shaping. Cut the top of the liner to conform to the scalloped top edge of the curtain, and hem the cut portions on the wrong side of the piece. Sew one of the washers to the apex of each scallop and one to the top of each tab, placing each approximately ½ inch down from the top and on the wrong side of the work. Snap the rings through both the liner and curtain. Tack the curtain to the liner if desired.

Japanese Floral Lid and Tank Cover

The Japanese character for *flower* is the predominant note on this rather unusual lid cover. Embroidered in a contrast color on a grospointed background, it is surrounded with an arrangement of small and large flowers, adding to the flavor of the design. The tank cover is purposely plain, made to coordinate with, but not distract from, the unique lid. Our set was made to fit one of the standard-size seats, the elongated type measuring 13½ inches at its widest point and 17½ inches at its longest. Since other standard sizes do exist, however, instructions are provided for adjusting the pattern.

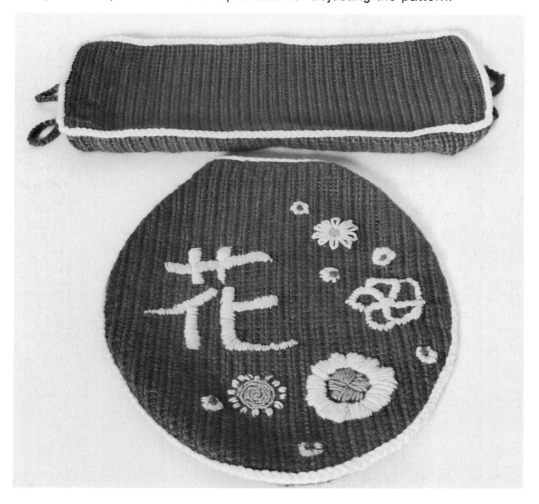

Materials:
2 pieces rug canvas, 7 spaces to 2 inches, one 16 × 23 inches for the lid cover
    and one 18 × 30 inches for the tank cover
masking tape
3 skeins (119 yards each) Reynolds Lopi, in purple
tapestry needle, #18
aluminum crochet hook, size H
small amounts Reynolds Reynelle in white, colonial, turquoise, and sunset
1¾ yards ribbon, 1 inch wide, in white

The Lid Cover

Cut the canvas for the lid piece according to Chart A, adding 3 extra spaces on all sides of the canvas beyond the number of spaces indicated on the chart.

Chart A

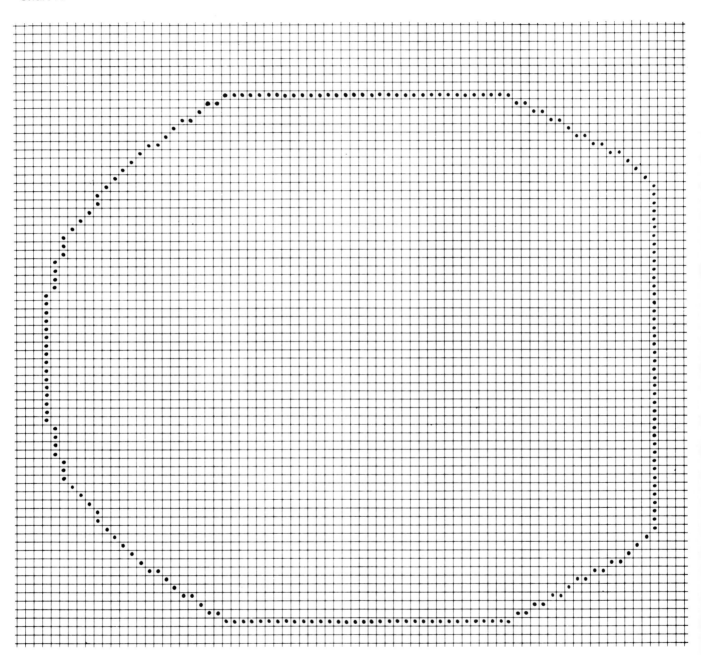

For a piece to cover a lid of a different size or shape, cut a paper pattern the size of the lid to be covered and cut the canvas to that size, again adding 3 extra spaces on all sides of the canvas beyond the actual size of your pattern.

Bind the edges of the canvas with masking tape. Then with double strands of Lopi, cover it, excluding the 3 extra spaces cut on each side, with the Kalem stitch. When this portion of the work has been completed, with the Lopi work 1 rnd of sc around the four sides of the embroidered piece, working enough sts so that the work lies flat and working these sts around through the last row of the embroidered canvas; fasten off. Now, with the right side of the work facing, attach the white yarn to the crocheted corner st at the top of the right-side edge of the piece and work 1 row of sc around three sides of the piece, eliminating the back portion, decreasing 1 st in every fifth st around, and working these sts through the back lps only of the crocheted sts on the previous row. Fasten off yarn and then attach it once more in the same st as that in which the last row was started. Work another row around, decreasing 1 st in every tenth st on this row and again working through the back lps of the sts. Now, following the color and stitch key on Chart B below, embroider the piece, spacing the sts as necessary if the size of your lid cover differs from ours.

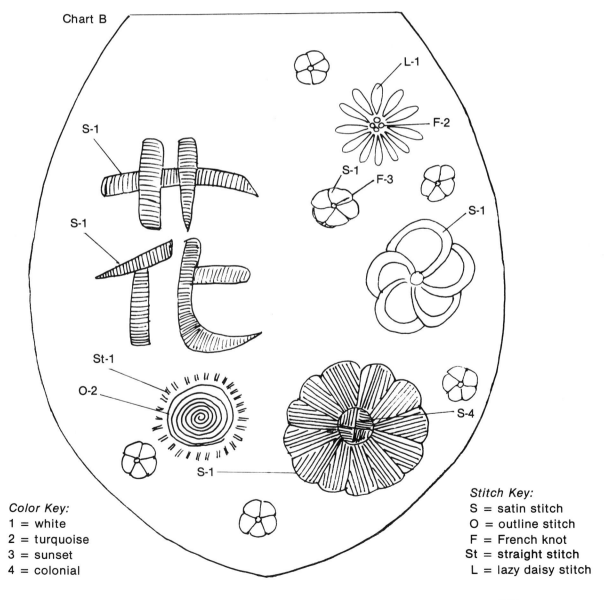

Chart B

Color Key:
1 = white
2 = turquoise
3 = sunset
4 = colonial

Stitch Key:
S = satin stitch
O = outline stitch
F = French knot
St = straight stitch
L = lazy daisy stitch

Finishing: Place the piece on your seat and mark out with pins it contour at the point where it begins to curve down to the underside. Then with double strands of white, crochet a chain to fit around this contoured line, adding enough ch sts to cover the back portion too. Sew this chain in place. Then cut away all excess unembroidered canvas around the edges, cover the cutaway edges by sewing the ribbon over it, and then with the Lopi make two chains of 50 sts each and sew one onto the left and right top edges of the white sc rows. Attach to the seat by tying the chains together behind the back of the seat.

The Tank Cover

Cut the canvas for this piece according to the diagram, adding 3 spaces

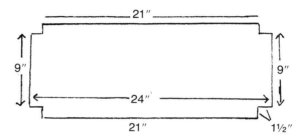

around the four sides of the piece. If your tank differs in size or shape from ours, again you must cut a paper pattern and cut the canvas to that size, adding 3 extra spaces on each of the four sides. To miter the corners, cut into the four corners of the piece as indicated on the chart. Now grospoint the piece with Lopi and the Kalem stitch as on the lid cover, covering the entire piece with the exception of the 3 extra spaces on each of the four sides. When this has been done, measure around the top outer edge of the piece, before the contoured drop, and with double strands of white, crochet a chain to fit around it. Sew the chain in place. Cut ribbon to fit around the four yet-unconnected dropped portions of the cover. Sew the top of each piece to the inside edge of each of the four sides of the cover. Now with the Lopi, crochet two chains, each long enough to extend 13 inches at each side beyond that amount necessary to insert the cord from the center of one short end to the center of the opposite end. Place each of these cords close to the sewn-on edge of the ribbon, each end extending 13 inches beyond the middle of the short-end sides of the cover. Sew on the unattached edge of the ribbon, leaving a small area open on each short-edge side for drawing the inserted chains through the ribbon; then sew the cut, mitered edges in place. Place on top of the tank, draw the Lopi chains from the center out toward each end so that the piece fits snugly, and tie two of the cord ends into a bow at either side of the piece.

118

Barefoot Fun

Big and small and different sizes and shapes of feet, including two of Spot's paws, are appliquéd onto a store-bought bathmat for a practical but fun piece in the bathroom. Yours can be as large a mat as you have need for and can have as many feet in different sizes and shapes "running around" as there are members of the household. After reading the simple instructions for ours, you may want to design your own personalized mat, made to include the feet of every member of your family and perhaps even imprints of your dog's, your cat's, and maybe even your canary's, feet. If not, we've included patterns for the feet on our rug.

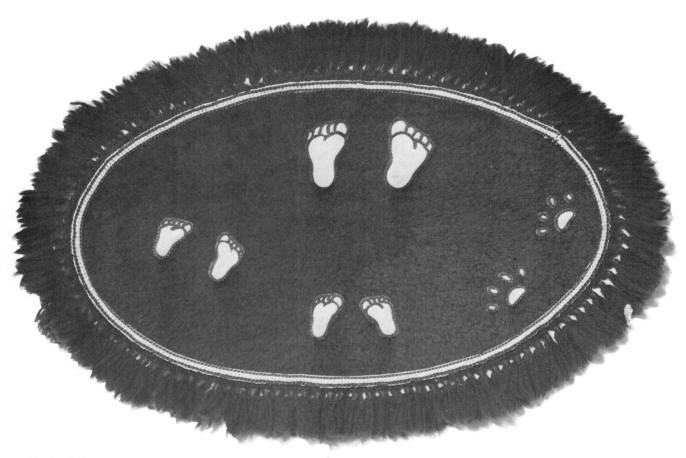

Materials:
tracing paper
carbon paper
small amount of felt, in white
1 ball (100 yards) Coats & Clark's "Speed-Cro-Sheen" in devil red (A) and
    1 ball in white (B)
tapestry needle, #18
small amount of bonding net
an oval, fringed mat, 17 × 29 inches, in brown
aluminum crochet hook, size D

The Mat

Using the tracing paper, trace one each of the larger feet, two each of the small feet, and two of Spot's paws. (*Note:* If you choose to use your own

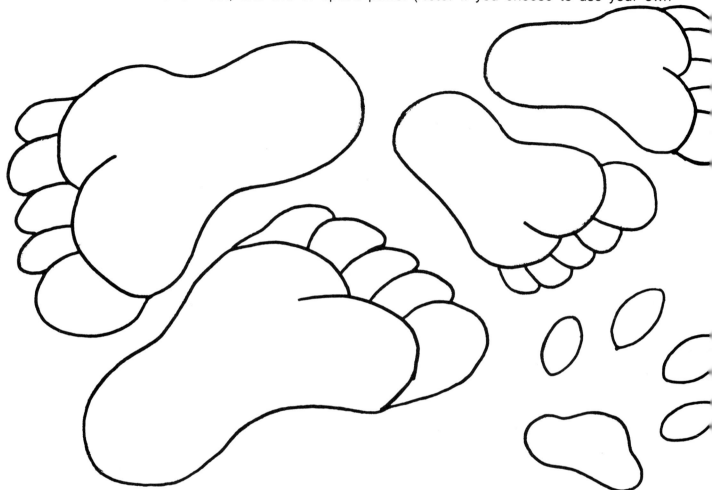

family's imprints, make patterns by placing each foot on a piece of white paper. Then draw around the shapes.) Pin the tracings to the felt over carbon paper placed face down and draw over the lines. Cut out the felt feet, adding 3/8- to ½-inch allowance on all sides. Remove the paper tracings. Then, with A, embroider a running chain stitch along the lines on the felt, making your stitches so that they will cover the 3/8 to ½ inch of the felt that extends beyond the traced lines. Cut a piece of bonding net for each foot cut, using the felt feet as patterns. Arrange the pieces as shown in the photograph or as desired on the mat and slip the appropriate piece of bonding net underneath. Following the instructions accompanying the package of net, apply the pieces. To finish the trimming of the mat, crochet a narrow edging around it, just within the fringed border, as follows: With B, make a chain long enough to fit completely around the portion to be trimmed. Then turn and work 1 sc in each st across. Break off B, attach A, turn, and work a sl st in each st. Fasten off A and, finally, attach B, turn, and work a sl st in each st across. Fasten off and then sew the edging in place as shown in the photograph, joining the short ends together.

Knitted Fingertip Towels

Richly textured, soft and absorbent, and easily and quickly made with a simple knit stitch and double strands of a medium-weight crochet cotton, our four fingertip towels are suitable for the most discerning of guests. Since they're also machine-washable, they're equally good for children's hasty hand washings. Make them in a color to match the color scheme of your bathroom, or do as we did and use a pristine white.

Materials:
14 balls (100 yards each) Coats & Clark's "Speed-Cro-Sheen," in white
2 pairs straight knitting needles, #6 and #10
steel crochet hook, #00

Pattern Stitch: *Row 1:* *Sl 1 st as if to p, k 1, yo, psso the k 1 and the yo, rep from * across the row. *Rows 2 and 4:* P. *Row 3:* K 1, *sl 1 st as if to p, k 1, yo, psso the k 1 and the yo, rep from * across, and end k 1. Repeat Rows 1 through 4 for pattern.

Gauge in Pattern Stitch: 5 stitches = 1 inch

The Towels

With double strands of yarn and #6 needles, cast on 54 sts. K 1 row, p 1 row, then k 1 more row. Change to #10 needles and pat st, and continuing to work with double yarn to completion, work even in pat st for 16 inches. Now change to #6 needles and p 1 row, k 1 row, and p 1 row. Bind off tightly.

Finishing: With double strands of yarn and the crochet hook, work an edging along each short edge of the towels as follows: With right side of work facing, attach yarn in the corner st, *ch 6, sk 1 st, sl st in the next st, rep from * across the row, and end with a sl st in the last st. Fasten off.

Mirror-Framed Bright Flowers and a
Matching After-Bath Sarong

Your own bright flowers, cut to the patterns below, reembroidered, and adhered to a terry hand towel, add a handsome note to your bathroom wall when framed in 4-inch-square self-adhesive mirror tiles. And for extra luxury, trim a larger towel with the same flowers and a simple crocheted edging to make an after-bath sarong.

Materials:

½ yard washable variegated fabric in warm pink shades (A), ½ yard in medium lilac shades (B), and ½ yard in leaf green shades (C)

embroidery hoop, approximately 6½ inches in diameter

2 skeins (9 yards each) J. & P. Coats Deluxe Six Strand Embroidery Floss in emerald green (A), 2 skeins in chartreuse (B), 2 skeins in yellow (C), 2 skeins in black (D), and 2 skeins in white (E)

sharp-pointed embroidery needle

needle and thread, in colors to match fabrics

terry hand towel, approximately 15 × 20 inches, in white (for the wall hanging)

approximately ½ yard medium-weight bonding net

white glue

1 piece plywood, ¼ inch thick, 20 × 24 inches

18 self-adhesive mirror tiles, each 4 inches square

2 screw eyes and a length of fine wire (for hanging)

terry bath towel, approximately 26 × 47 inches, in white (for the sarong)

steel crochet hook, #00

3 balls (100 yards each) Coats & Clark's "Speed-Cro-Sheen," in emerald

2 small white buttons

1 snap fastener

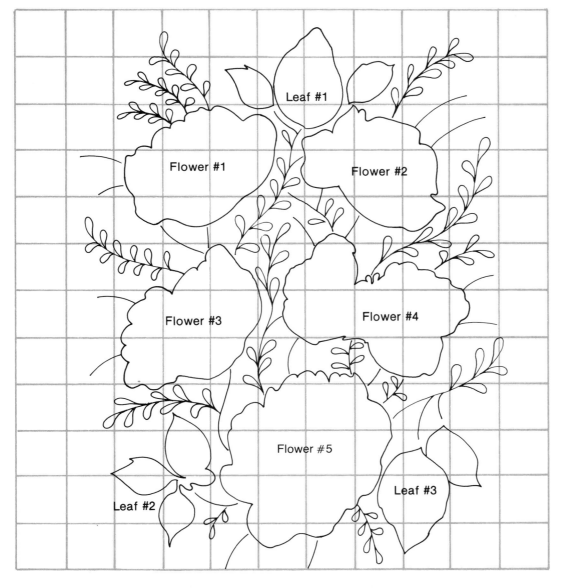

Loops for leaves are worked in lazy daisy stitch in emerald "Speed-Cro-Sheen" Stems are worked in outline stitch in emerald "Speed-Cro-Sheen"

each square = 1 inch

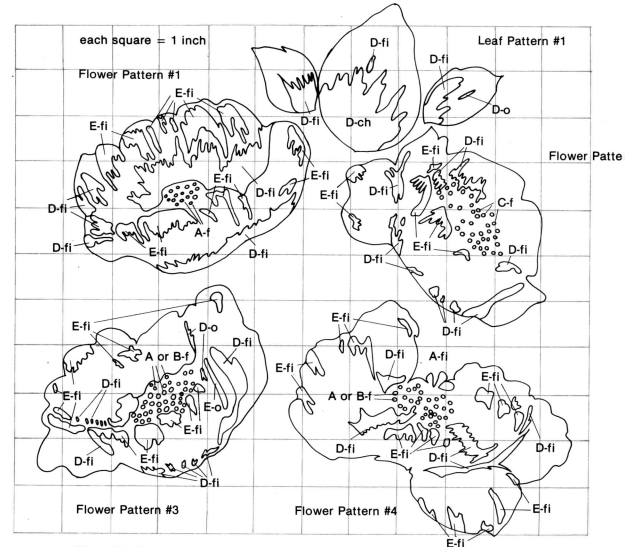

each square = 1 inch

Flower Pattern #1

Leaf Pattern #1

Flower Patte

Flower Pattern #3

Flower Pattern #4

The Wall Hanging

Enlarge and transfer each of the five flower and three leaf patterns onto the variegated fabrics. Use the pink and lilac fabrics for the flowers and the green for the leaves. Then cut around the tracings, leaving ample fabric on all sides so that the pieces will set into your embroidery hoop. Now following the color and stitch key, embroider each piece as shown. When this has been done, trim around each piece, allowing enough extra fabric to make a ¼-inch hem. Sew the hems and then arrange the pieces on the hand towel, following the chart for the arrangement. Adhere them to the towel with the bonding net, cuttting the net to the shape of each piece and adhering each according to the instructions accompanying the net. Finally, when the design has been set, use the "Speed-Cro-Sheen" to embroider leaves and stems between the flowers, as shown on the chart on page 123. Work the stems in outline stitch and the small leaves in the lazy daisy stitch.

Finishing: Glue the towel to the plywood and then press the mirror tiles in place around the four sides of the board, making sure that the outer edges of the tiles are flush with the outer edges of the board. For hanging, insert the two screw eyes into the back of the board and thread them with the necessary amount of wire for the desired hanging position.

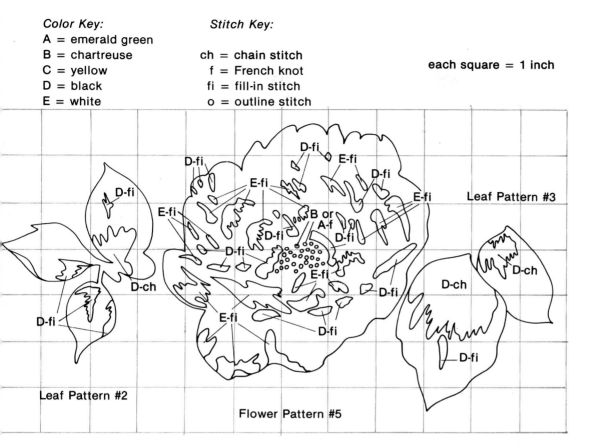

Leaf Pattern #3

Leaf Pattern #2

Flower Pattern #5

The Sarong

Enlarge, transfer, and cut the flowers and leaves in the same way as you did
for the wall hanging. Then adhere them in the same arrangement onto the right
side of the bath towel, using the length of the towel for the wraparound portion
and centering the arrangement so that the furthermost part of it is 4 inches in
from the end and the uppermost part 4 inches down from the top. Embroider
the stems directly onto the towel, as you did for the hanging. Then crochet an
edging around the four sides of the piece as follows: With the right side of the
towel facing and working the crochet hook directly into the towel, start in any
corner and sc into the corner, *ch 6, sk ¾ of an inch, sc into the material, rep
from * around the four edges, and end with a sl st in the first st. Do not turn.
Next rnd: *Sc, dc, and sc in the ch-6 lp, sl st in the next sc, rep from * around.
Fasten off. For each of the straps, ch 7 and work in sc on 6 sts for 13 inches or
the desired length so that the straps fit comfortably over the shoulders. Then
work 1 row of sc along each side edge of the straps and, finally, a second row
of edging along the four sides of the straps as you did around the four sides of
the towel itself. Sew the short ends of the straps to the front and back of the
sarong, pinning them first in place so that they are in the proper position. Wrap
the piece around your body and mark where the overlap should be fastened for
a good fit. On the left side, sew one button at the top and the other 9 inches
down from the top, both along the mark you have made. Try the piece on again
and mark the position for the snap fastener so that the underneath corner at
the top will hold neatly in place. Sew on the fastener.

The Flower-Embroidered Area Rug and Matching Wall Hanging

Partly latch-hooked, partly grospointed, and partly reembroidered, this charming 25-inch-in-diameter area rug and 11- by 16-inch framed wall hanging will add an enchanting note to any room in your home. We've designed the set for the bathroom, but it would do as well in your daughter's room or as a lovely note in your own bedroom, the rug alongside the bed and the small hanging placed on the wall just above the headboard. Choose your colors, of course, to match the color of the room in which you will be using it.

Materials:
2 pieces rug canvas, 7 spaces to 2 inches, 26 inches square for the rug and
    14 × 16½ inches for the wall hanging
masking tape
6 skeins (119 yards each) Reynolds Lopi, in purple #83
tapestry needle, #18
latchet hook
needle and thread, in purple
2 yards iron-on rug binding, 1½ inches wide
small amounts Reynolds Reynelle in white, colonial, turquoise, light lime, and
    sunset
cardboard mat, 8 × 11 inches (inside measurement), in white
picture frame, ¾ inch wide, 11 × 16 inches, in white

The Rug

Bind the edges of the piece of canvas for the rug with masking tape. Then, using double strands of Lopi, the tapestry needle, and the Kalem stitch, work the center grospointed portion of the rug, following the chart for the portion of the canvas to be filled in. When this part of the rug has been completed, work the

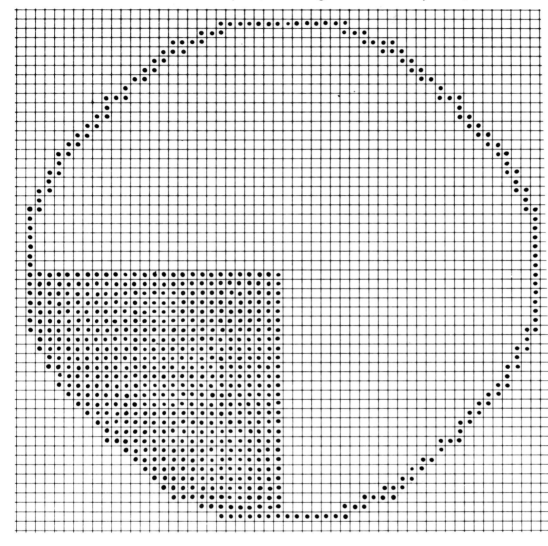

Working in the Kalem stitch, repeat the filled-in segment three times more around to complete the circle.

latched portion, following the contour of the inner circle and working, with double strands of yarn, 1 st in every st on every other row of the canvas until there are just 3 spaces left unworked at the four widest parts of the circle. Round the four corner points by cutting away the excess canvas beyond the 3 spaces. Turn the 3 unworked rows to the underside, clipping and folding the canvas to take in the excess material along the curved edges, and sew the hem in place. Complete the underside of the piece by covering the hem with rug binding. Finally, with single strands of yarn and the embroidery needle, embroider the grospointed center of the rug, following the color and stitch keys.

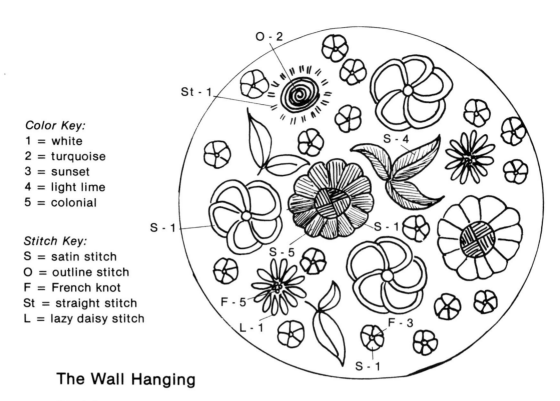

Color Key:
1 = white
2 = turquoise
3 = sunset
4 = light lime
5 = colonial

Stitch Key:
S = satin stitch
O = outline stitch
F = French knot
St = straight stitch
L = lazy daisy stitch

The Wall Hanging

Bind the edges of the remaining piece of canvas with masking tape. Then, with double strands of Lopi, grospoint the piece with the Kalem stitch, leaving 3 spaces of the canvas unworked on each of the four sides of the canvas. When this has been completed, embroider the piece with the flowers as shown on the chart. Then frame it as we did with the mat and white frame, or in any other way you prefer.

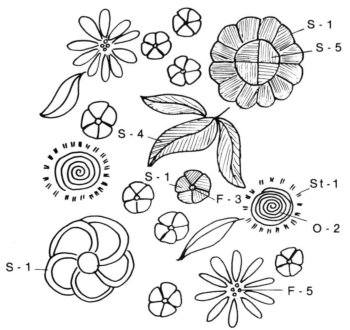

128

AND THE PATIO AND THE GARDEN

The Barbecue Butler

Amateur, and certainly more experienced, outdoor cooks will welcome a handy container like this one, with space and provision for all the tools and accoutrements necessary for preparing a super feast, no matter whether the *plat du jour* is to be a simple string of hot dogs or, more formally, a roast slowly turning on the spit. Our own cleverly contrived hanging butler, made of clear-plastic-covered knitted pockets mounted onto a sheet of plywood, has room for absolutely everything, including the barbecue mitt, the spatula and large spoon, perhaps a big knife and fork and basting brush, other tools one might choose to have handy, and every possible seasoning and condiment needed or wanted for doing a really top-notch job.

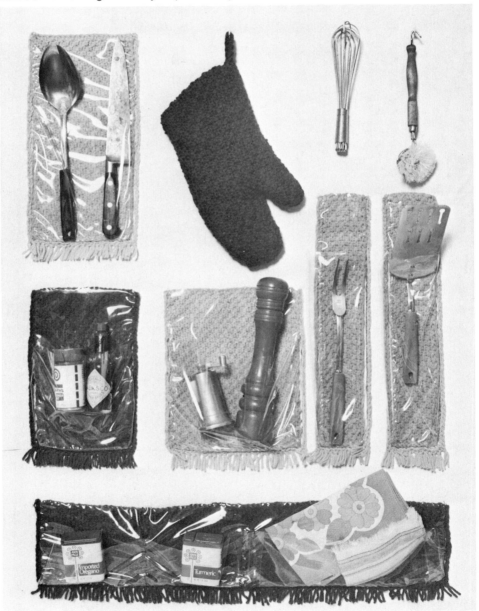

Materials:
2 skeins (4 ounces each) Spinnerin 4-ply Orlon acrylic in burgundy (A),
    1 skein in aqua (B), 1 skein in hunter green (C), and 1 skein in lime (D)
1 pair straight knitting needles, #10
stitch holder
needle and thread, in burgundy and clear nylon
small amount of washable fabric (for mitt lining)
aluminum crochet hook, size G
1 yard medium-weight clear plastic, 36 inches wide
1 yard vinyl, 45 inches wide, in white
wood staple gun
1 piece plywood, ¼ inch thick, 28 × 38 inches
4 yards masking tape, 1½ inches wide
3 cup hooks, in white
white glue

Pattern Stitch: *Row 1:* *K 1, p 1, rep from * across the row. *Row 2:* K the sts that were purled on the previous row and p the sts that were knitted. *Row 3:* *P 1, k 1, rep from * across the row. *Row 4:* Rep Row 2. Repeat Rows 1 through 4 for the pattern stitch.

Gauge in Pattern Stitch: 7 stitches = 2 inches

The Butler

Pockets: Pocket A: With B, cast on 22 sts. Work even in pat st for 13 inches and then bind off in k. Pocket B: With C, cast on 22 sts. Work even in pat st for 10 inches and then bind off in k. Pocket C: With B, cast on 28 sts. Work even in pat st for 10 inches and bind off as for the others. Work pockets D and E again as for the others, working both of these on 10 sts with color D for 16 inches; for pocket F, work with color A on 84 sts for 5 inches.

Mitt: Starting at the top, cast on 37 sts with color A and work even in pat st for 1 inch. Then, continuing to maintain the pat as established, inc 1 st at beg and end of every other row until there are 45 sts. Work even on 45 sts until piece measures 8 inches in all. Then shape first half of thumb: Inc 1 st in the first st, work across the next 6 sts, then sl the remaining sts on a holder and work back and forth on the 8 sts on the needle for 2 inches. Now dec 1 st at beg and end of the next row, work 1 row even, and bind off. Sl the first 31 sts from the holder onto a needle and work in pat st on these sts for 3 inches. Then dec 1 st at beg and end of every other row twice. When 27 sts remain, work 1 row even and bind off. Work the remaining 7 sts to correspond to the first half of thumb, reversing the shaping. To finish this piece, cut two pieces of lining material to conform to the shape of the mitt and sew them in place. Finally, sew all the open seams on the piece. For a hanging loop, attach double strands of A to the top of the seam, ch 10, join with a sl st to the next st after the seam stitch, and fasten off.

Finishing: Finish each of the six pockets with a row of 1-inch-long self-color fringe across the bottom of it, knotting one 3-inch strand in every other st across the last row of the knitting. Now cut pieces of clear plastic to fit over

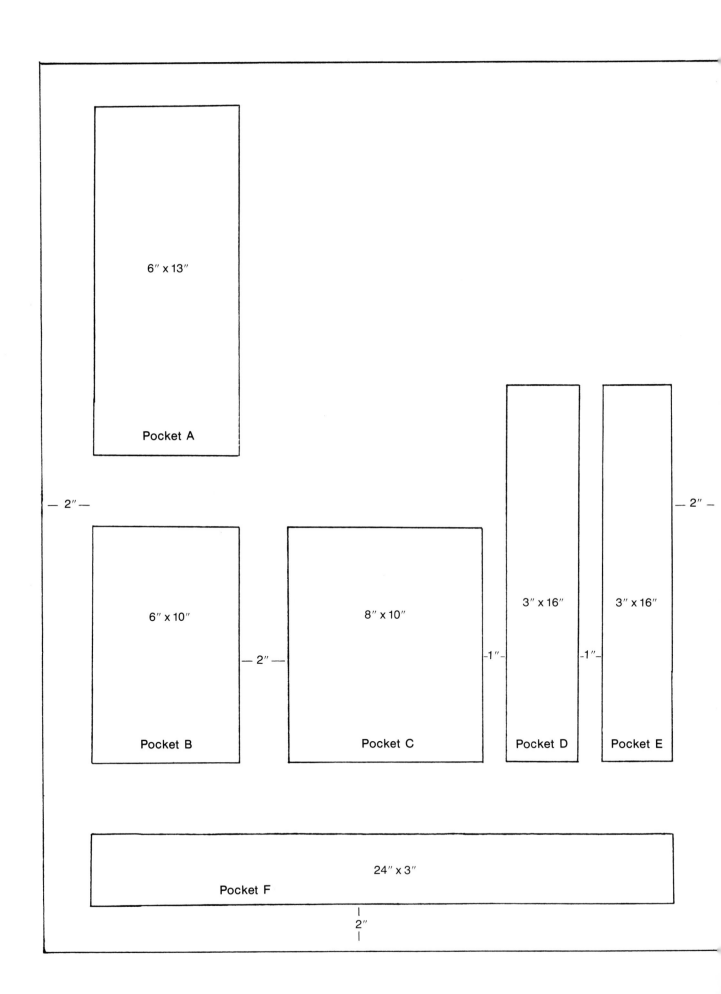

6″ x 13″

Pocket A

— 2″ —

6″ x 10″

8″ x 10″

3″ x 16″

3″ x 16″

— 2″ —

Pocket B

— 2″ —

Pocket C

-1″-

Pocket D

-1″-

Pocket E

24″ x 3″

Pocket F

2″

each of the six knitted pieces and, with nylon thread, sew the plastic over the pieces. Cut the vinyl 3 inches larger all around than the plywood. Mark out on the vinyl the position of the pockets. Then, following the chart, sew the plastic-covered knitted pieces in place. Next, cut clear plastic pieces to make the pocket for each knitted piece. Cut each of these pieces so that it covers the lower two-thirds of each knitted piece, not including the fringe, and is 1½ inches wider than the knitted pieces on each side. With needle and thread, sew each pocket over the plastic-covered knitted pieces, sewing along the side edges, pleating in the extra 1½ inches on either side before sewing the bottoms, and leaving the top portions open so that the necessary accessories can fit into them. Divide the bottom pocket at the center, and stitch this division from top to bottom with thread. Finally, staple the vinyl over the plywood and adhere the edges with masking tape. Insert three cup hooks near the top of the board for the hanging of the mitt, the brush, and the hot dog "clip," or any other tools you may prefer. Then with the crochet hook, make six chains, each long enough to fit along both sides and across the bottom of each plastic-lined, plastic-covered pocket, using self-color yarn. Finally, glue the chains in place around the pockets.

A Decorative Shield for Outdoor Hors d'Oeuvres

This miniature transparent umbrella would be an exceptionally charming decorative accessory even if it did not serve such a functional purpose—keeping the bugs and dust out. Simply made by appliquéing the top portion of a child's clear plastic umbrella with a number of crisp, white hairpin-lace motifs, it will protect your outdoor setup of party foods until the guests arrive and even after, when nothing remains but leftovers.

Materials:
4 balls (1 ounce each) Spinnerin Elf in white (MC) and 1 ball in bright green (CC)
adjustable hairpin-lace loom
aluminum crochet hook, size C
a child's clear plastic umbrella, approximately 25 inches in bottom diameter
handsaw
needle and nylon thread
white glue

The Shield

Motifs (Make forty-two): With the loom adjusted to 1 inch and using MC, work 16 lps on each side, having the spine of the piece ¼ inch in from one outside edge. Fasten off, leaving a length of thread measuring approximately 12 inches. Sew the spine ends together with this thread. Then draw the remainder of it tightly through the short lps of the piece, forming the center of a circle. Fasten off. To finish the outer edge of the circle, attach the yarn in any lp, *ch 2, sc in the next lp, rep from * around, and join the last st with a sl st to the first sc. Next rnd: Work 1 sc in each sc and 3 sc in each ch-2 lp around. Join the end of the rnd with a sl st and fasten off.

Finishing: Open the umbrella and saw through the handle portion just below the latch. Discard the lower part. Now arrange ten motifs along every other plastic section between spokes, placing them in pyramid fashion as shown. When these have been arranged, join them together as they are set, tacking them at the few points necessary to secure the arrangement. Finally, tack the top one and the four bottom ones to the plastic of the umbrella, tacking the top edge only of the top one and the bottom edges only of the others. Trim the finished piece as follows: With double strands of CC, crochet six chains, each long enough to fit from the top to the bottom of the six spokes of the umbrella. Glue these in place. Again with double strands of CC, crochet a chain long enough to fit around the bottom circumference of the open umbrella. Work a second row along this chain as follows: *Ch 10, sk 4 ch, sl st in the next ch, rep from * around, and fasten off. Glue this around the bottom of the umbrella. For a final trim, crochet three chains with double strands of CC, each approximately 10 inches long. Knot both ends of each chain, tie each into a bow, and glue one at the top of each clear portion of the piece, as shown.

A Bright Covering for Your Barbecue Grill

Gay Roman stripes add a colorful note to your outdoor setting, and the clear plastic over the covering is a good protective device against dust and rain. Crocheted in the round with multicolored strands of yarn on a large hook, the cover is easy and quick to make. Although ours was designed for a grill measuring 24½ inches in top diameter, it is a relatively simple matter to adjust the crocheting to fit whatever size you need, whether it be smaller or larger. Also, while we chose to cover ours with plastic so that it could be kept clean with just a damp cloth, you might prefer to omit the plastic and just throw the colorfast, machine-washable-and-dryable crocheted piece into the washer once it's become soiled.

Materials:
1 skein (4 ounces) Spinnerin 4-ply Orlon Acrylic in white (A), 1 skein in lime (B),
    1 skein in hunter green (C), 2 ounces in aqua (D), and 2 ounces in
    burgundy red (E)
aluminum crochet hook, size K
2 yards narrow elastic
2 yards medium-weight clear plastic (optional)
needle and nylon thread

Gauge: 5 stitches = 2 inches

The Cover

Starting at the center with A, ch 4 and join with a sl st to form a ring. Next rnd: Work 6 sc in the center of the ring. Next rnd: Work 2 sc in each sc around (12 sc). Break off A, attach B, and working in hdc, work *1 hdc in the next sc, 2 hdc in the next, rep from * around (18 hdc). Next rnd: With B and the hdc st, work *1 hdc in each of the next 2 hdc, 2 hdc in the next, rep from * around (24 hdc). Join the last st of this rnd to the first st and fasten off. Continue the work now as follows: Using the hdc st throughout, follow the color sequence of *2 rnds C, 1 rnd D, 1 rnd E, 2 rnds A, 2 rnds B, and rep from * to completion, increasing 6 sts evenly spaced on each rnd and having 1 st more between increases on each rnd until the piece measures approximately 24½ inches or the desired diameter. When changing the color of the yarn for the next rnd to be worked, always join the last st of the rnd just completed with a sl st to the first st of that rnd before fastening off, and attach the new color in the same st. When the desired diameter has been reached, continue with the hdc stitch and the color pattern, but work without increase for approximately 2½ inches more or to a size a little wider than the lip on your grill, crocheting the last rnd over a piece of elastic cut to fit around. If you choose to use the clear plastic, cut one piece to the diameter of the top of the cover before the even rnds were worked, and stitch this piece in place along the outer edge. Then cut another piece to fit around the circumference of the lip portion and about ½ inch wider than that part. Stitch the top edge of this piece to the outer edge of the large round piece, leaving the bottom of it open and unattached for flexibility.

A Set of Bright Placemats, Designed for Outdoor Dining

Broad green and white stripes, reembroidered with rows of daisies, add a gay note to any outdoor table setting. The mats, each of which measures 12 by 18 inches, are made of a crisp, machine-washable-and-dryable Creslan acrylic yarn worked in the simple single-crochet stitch.

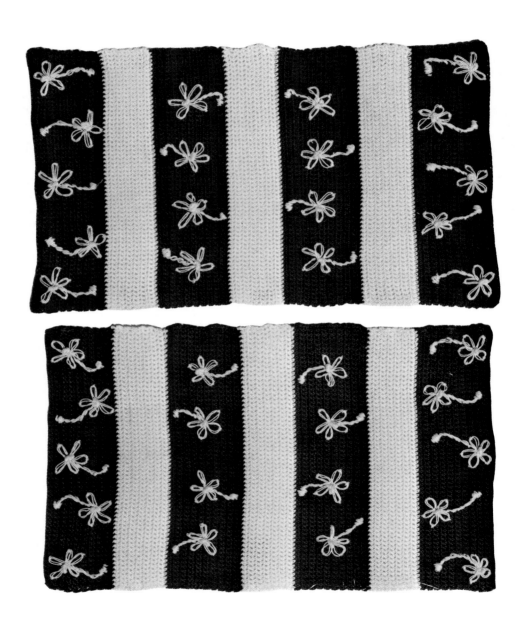

Materials:
7 balls (1 ounce each) Spinnerin Elf in bright green (A) and 4 balls in white (B)
    (for two mats)
aluminum crochet hook, size F
tapestry needle, #18

Gauge in Single Crochet: 9 stitches = 2 inches
                                  6 rows = 1 inch

The Placemats

Make two: With A, ch 55. Work even in sc on 54 sts for 3 inches. Continuing on these sts, *work with B for 2 inches and A for 3 inches. Rep from * twice more. Fasten off.

Finishing: With double strands of B, embroider five-petaled stemmed daisies along the color-A stripes as follows: Embroider five along each of the two outside stripes and four along each of the two center stripes, staggering the position of each group of five as shown in the photograph and working the groups of four in a straight line, placing each of these four midway between each of the daisies on the groups of five. Embroider the petals of the flowers with a lazy daisy stitch and the centers with a French knot. For the stems, use an outline stitch and a small finishing of satin stitches at the bottom of each.

A Green Grass Rug, Encircled with Colorful Flowers

Simply made yet simply elegant on any patio or terrace floor, our latchet-hooked "green grass" has an inside grospointed border trim onto which colorful crocheted flowers have been appliquéd. Measuring a total of 36 inches in diameter and worked on a broad 7-spaces-to-2-inch canvas, the effect is charming, especially considering the relatively small amount of work involved.

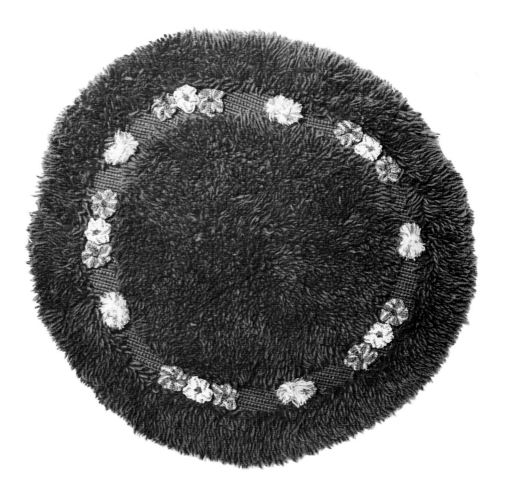

Materials:
1 piece rug canvas, 7 spaces to 2 inches, 38 inches square
masking tape
10 balls (50 grams each) Bernat Husky, in sage (MC)
latchet hook
blunt-ended embroidery needle
needle and thread, in green, red, and white
4 yards iron-on rug binding, 1½ inches wide
aluminum crochet hook, size D
2 skeins (1 ounce each) Bernat Carioca in ruby (A), 2 skeins in white (B), and
    1 skein in fuchsia (C)
small piece of cardboard
small amount of stuffing material (optional)

Barefoot Fun, p. 119; Knitted Fingertip Towels, p. 121. ▶

▲
Macraméd Fishnet, p. 111; A Hairpin-Lace Shower Curtain, p. 113.

Japanese Floral Lid and Tank Cover, p. 115; The Flower-Embroidered Area Rug and Matching Wall ▶
Hanging, p. 126.

The Rug

Rug: Bind the edges of the canvas with masking tape. For the latch-hooked portion of the rug, cut MC into 3¾-inch-long pieces. Then, starting at the center and following the chart, latch 1 st in every sp on every other row. When

sections between lines are worked one time only. The quarter between A and B is repeated four times in all to complete the circle.

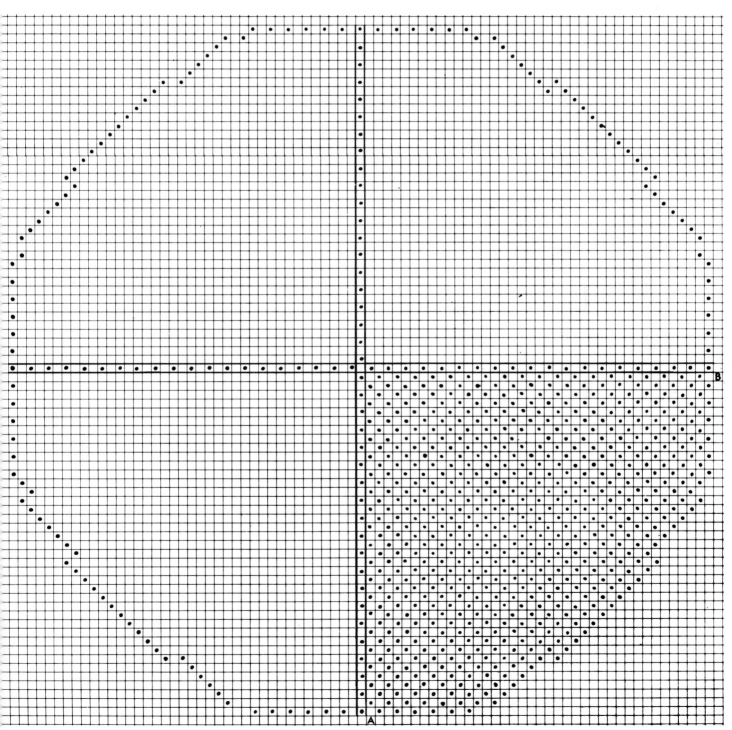

Mirror-Framed Bright Flowers and a Matching After-Bath Sarong, p. 122.

this part of the work has been completed, work in grospoint and the continental stitch for 3½ inches around the outer circumference of the latch-hooked portion. Finally, work with the latchet hook as before until there are just 3 spaces left unworked at the four widest parts of the circle. Round the four corner points now by cutting away the excess canvas beyond the 3 spaces. Turn the 3 unworked rows under to make a hem, clipping and folding the canvas to take in the excess material along the curved edges. Sew the hem in place and complete the underside of the piece by covering the hem with rug binding.

Flowers: Make ten 5-petaled flowers with A as the main color and five with B as the main color as follows: For each petal of the color-A flowers, ch 6 with A, dc in the third ch from hook, hdc in the next, sc in the next, and 2 sc in the last. Then, working along the opposite side of the ch, work 1 sc, 1 hdc, and 2 dc. Drop A, pick up B, turn, and with B, work 2 sc in the same st, 1 sc in each of the next 3 sts, 3 sc in the corner st, and 1 sc in each of the next 4 sts. Cut B, pick up A, and turn. Work the last row with A as follows: Work 2 sc in the same st, 1 sc in each of the next 4 sts, 3 sc in the corner st, and 1 sc in each of the next 5 sts. Now, with A, gather together the one remaining straight side edge of the petal by drawing up 3 lps evenly spaced across that edge, then placing the yarn over the hook, and drawing it through the 4 lps. Fasten off. Make a total of fifty petals in this way. To finish each of the color-A flowers, overlap one end of each of the five petals to form a circle, join the overlapped portions with an overcast st, and then, with MC, embroider 5 overcast sts in the center joining. Make the remaining five color-B flowers in the same manner, substituting B for A and A for B. To make each of the five "carnation" pompoms, wrap one strand each of A, B, and C 30 times around a 3-inch-wide strip of cardboard. Cut through the strands at one end, tie them around the center, and fluff the strands into a pompom. Trim the ends evenly.

Finishing: Arrange the petaled flowers into five groups of three flowers each—two color-A flowers with one color-B between—evenly spaced over the grospointed portion of the rug. Tack the flowers in position, stuffing each lightly if desired. Then arrange the "carnations" evenly spaced between the other groupings and tack those in place.

The Windmobile

Here, seven macramé cords of varying lengths have been strung with large multicolored wooden beads to lend a breezy note to your home, either indoors or out. Our windmobile, designed with flowery pink hues and rich leaf greens, sways and dances outdoors, gently with a soft breeze and a little more vigorously when the wind blows a little harder.

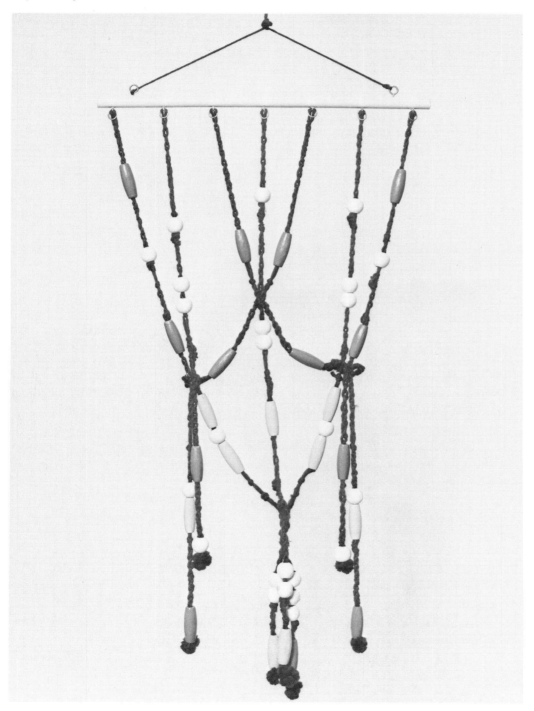

Materials:
dowel rod, 1 inch in diameter, 18 inches long
1 small spray can enamel, in white
9 screw eyes
1 ball (4 ounces) Bernat Big Berella Bulky, in hunter green
24 round wooden beads, approximately 3 inches in diameter, in white (A);
      13 cylindrical beads, approximately 2½ inches in diameter and 2 inches
      in length, in deep pink (B); 9 cylindrical beads of the same size in light pink
      (C) (*Note:* If the beads are not available in colors, paint them. This is best
      done by stringing each group to be sprayed a particular color on a piece
      of cord and spraying them all at one time.)
needle and thread, in green

The Windmobile

Spray the dowel white. Then screw seven of the screw eyes evenly spaced across the bottom of it. Screw the two remaining screw eyes in place on top of the dowel, each one midway between the two end hooks on either side of the bottom. Cut a strand of yarn that is the desired length for a hanging cord, thread it through the two top screw eyes, and tie the ends securely together at the center. Cut seven lengths of yarn, each 150 inches long. Using the dowel and the bottom screw eyes and following the general macramé instructions, make seven half-square-knotted cords, each strung with beads. To start each of the cords, fold one strand of yarn in half, thread it through one of the screw eyes, and work as follows: Cords #1 and #7: Working all cords with half square knots, work for 7 inches, string one B bead, make a double slipknot to hold the bead in place, work 2½ inches, string one A bead, slipknot, and then continuing to alternate cords and beads with a slipknot after each bead, work 1½ inches, one B, 3½ inches, one A, 3 inches, one C, 3 inches, and one B. Tie a heavy slipknot at the bottom of these two cords. Then complete them by making two small pompoms of green yarn and sewing one at the bottom of each, just below the last B bead. Cords #2 and #6: Alternating macramé cords and beads as above, work now in the following sequence: 5 inches of half square knots, then one A bead, 6½ inches and one A, 1 inch, one A, 3 inches, one C, 1 inch, one A, 1 inch, one C, 2½ inches, and one A, 1 inch, one A, 1½ inches, and one C. Finish these cords with a heavy slipknot at the bottom and two pompoms as for cords #1 and #7. Cords #3 and #5: Working as for the other cords, knot 7½ inches of the cord, then slip one B bead, work 6 inches and add another B, work 4½ inches and slip on a third B, and, finally, work 4 inches and add one A. Finish these two cords as the others. Cord #4: Continuing as for the other cords, work 3½ inches, slip one A, 9 inches, one A, 1 inch, one A, 4 inches, one C, 5½ inches, one A, 1 inch, one A, 1 inch, one A, 2 inches, and one B. Again secure and trim the bottom of this cord with a slipknot and a pompom.

Finishing: Twist the cords according to the following chart and, with needle and thread, tack them in place at all joining points shown.

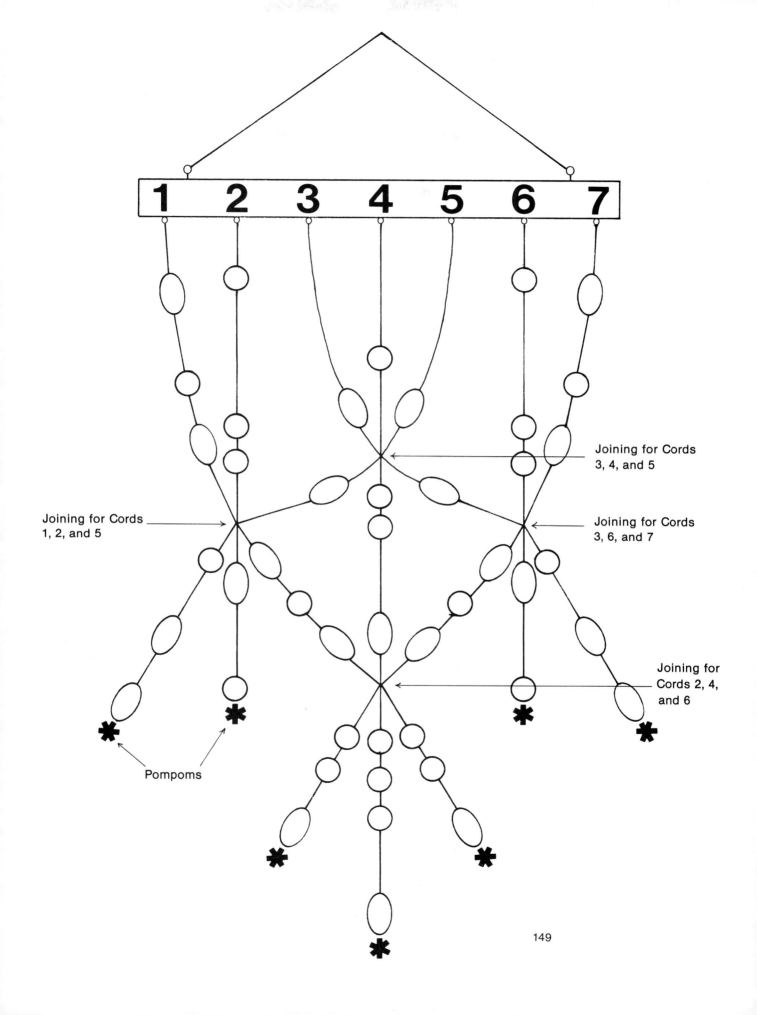

Joining for Cords
3, 4, and 5

Joining for Cords
1, 2, and 5

Joining for Cords
3, 6, and 7

Joining for
Cords 2, 4,
and 6

Pompoms

149

Colorful Crocheted Containers for Potted and Rooting Plants

Three-colored textured stripes add an interesting note to containers for potted or rooting plants. For our arrangement, we've made five baskets for potted plants, three of which are designed to stand and two to hang, and we've added one piece to cover an empty wine bottle into which we've set a rooting plant. The containers add a decorative note to a terrace or patio setting, and there are many ways of grouping them, one of which might be to place them within the empty spaces formed by a "catacomb" arrangement of seven or nine 8-inch concrete cinder blocks, using the blocks either in their natural color or sprayed white.

Materials:
2 balls (1 4/10 ounces each) Unger Cruise in red #44 (A) and 2 balls in white #60 (B)
3 skeins (20 grams each) Unger Ariane, in pink #2 (C)
aluminum crochet hook, size G
needle and thread, in white
5 plastic flowerpots, each approximately 6 inches in diameter and 5¼ inches high, in white
1 empty wine bottle, approximately 3 inches in diameter and 11½ inches high, with a 3-inch neck

Pattern Stitch: *Row 1*: With A, ch 2, (3 dc, ch 1, 3 dc) in third ch from hook, *sk 2 ch, 1 sc in next ch, sk 2 ch, (3 dc, ch 1, 3 dc) in next ch (shell made), rep from * across and end 1 sc in last ch, turn. *Row 2*: With B, ch 3, 2 dc in first sc, *sk 3 dc, 1 sc in next ch-1 sp, sk 3 dc, 1 shell in next sc, rep from * across and end 3 dc in turning ch of previous row, turn. *Row 3*: With C, ch 2, *sk 3 dc, 1 shell in next sc, sk 3 dc, 1 sc in next ch-1 sp, rep from * across and end sk 2 dc, 1 sc in turning ch of previous row, turn. Repeat Rows 2 and 3 for pattern, alternating colors A, B, and C on every row.

Gauge in Single Crochet: 4 stitches = 1 inch

The Pot Covers

Make three baskets for the standing plants in the following way: With A, ch 76 and then work even in pat st for approximately 4½ inches, ending with a color-B row. Fasten off yarn and sew the short ends together. Then, with B, work 1 rnd of sc around the top of the piece, working 1 sc in each dc and in each sc around; fasten off. With A, work 1 rnd of sc around the bottom of the piece, working 1 sc in each st of the starting chain; fasten off. For the two hanging baskets, work in the same manner as for the other three except to finish as follows: When the top of the piece has been completed, work color-A sc in each st of the starting chain. Next rnd: Work even in sc on 76 sts. Next rnd: Work 2 sts tog around (38 sts). Next rnd: Work even in sc on 38 sts. Next rnd: Work 2 sts tog around (19 sts). Next rnd: Work even in sc on 19 sts. Next rnd: Work 2 sts tog around, ending with 1 sc in the last st (10 sts). Last rnd: Work 2 sts tog around (5 sts). Break off yarn, leaving a length of thread. Draw the thread tightly through the remaining stitches and fasten off. To complete these baskets for hanging: With double strands of B, make two chains of 200 sts for each of the two baskets. Puncture four evenly spaced holes around the top of each of the two pots, approximately ¾ inch below the top. Using two chains for each of these baskets, thread one chain through one hole, going from the inside of the pot out and making a knot on the inside of the threaded chain to hold it in place, and then thread the opposite end of that chain from the outside toward the inside in the hole directly opposite the one with the original threading. Again knot this end on the inside. Then thread one more of the chains in the same manner through the two remaining holes in the pot. Finally, knot the two top loops of the two chains into one hanging loop of the desired size.

The Bottle Cover

For the cover for the bottle, work as follows: With A, ch 40. Work even in pat st for 7½ inches, ending with a color-A row. Fasten off. Then sew the short ends together. Attach A again to the top of the piece and, working around in sc, work even on 40 sts for each of the next 2 rnds. Next rnd: Work 2 sc tog across the first 12 sts, then 1 sc in each of the next 16 sts, and 2 sc tog across the last 12 sts (28 sts). Next rnd: Work 2 sts tog around (14 sts). Work even now on 14 sts for 3¾ inches; fasten off. To complete this piece, work 1 row of color A around the bottom, as on the other pieces, working 1 sc in each st of the starting chain.

"HOW-TO" STITCH EXPLANATIONS

Crochet

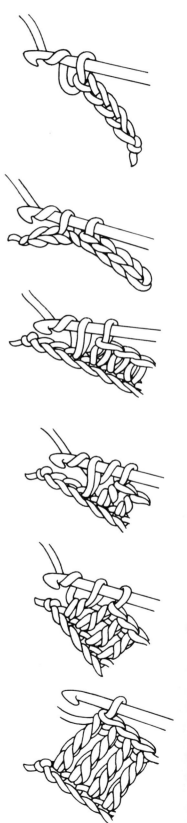

Foundation Chain

Knot a loop onto the hook. Holding the hook in your right hand and the end of the yarn extending from the loop between the thumb and middle finger of your left hand, loop the yarn to be worked over the index finger of your left hand. The balance of that yarn should extend from the same hand, lightly held in control between the ring and little fingers. Then *pass the hook under the extending yarn nearest to the hook and draw both the hook and the yarn through the loop already on the hook (the first stitch). Repeat from * for as many stitches as the instructions specify. (Note: Turning chains are worked in the same way as are chain stitches indicated in a pattern stitch—the last loop worked is the one through which the yarn and hook of the next stitch are drawn.)

Slip Stitch

Insert the hook through the two upper strands of the stitch to be worked, place the yarn over the hook, and then draw both yarn and the hook through the stitch and through the last loop on the hook.

Single Crochet

Insert the hook through the two upper strands of the stitch to be worked, place the yarn over the hook and draw it through the stitch, then yarn over again and draw it through the remaining two loops on the hook. When working the first row of the single crochet on a foundation chain, start your first stitch in the second chain from the hook and always chain 1 to turn when the first stitch on the next row is to be a single crochet.

Half Double Crochet

Place the yarn over the hook and then insert the hook through the two upper strands of the stitch to be worked. Draw the yarn through the stitch, yarn over again, and draw it through the remaining three loops on the hook. When working the first row of half double crochet on a foundation chain, start your first stitch in the third chain from the hook and always chain 2 to turn when the first stitch on the next row is to be a half double crochet.

Double Crochet

Place the yarn over the hook and then insert the hook through the two upper strands of the stitch to be worked. Draw the yarn through the stitch, yarn over, draw it through two loops on the hook, yarn over again, and draw it through the remaining two loops on the hook. When working the first row of double crochet on a foundation chain, start your first stitch in the third chain from the hook and always chain 2 to turn when the first stitch on the next row is to be a double crochet.

Treble Crochet

Place the yarn twice over the hook and then insert the hook through the two upper strands of the stitch to be worked. Draw the yarn through the stitch, place the yarn over the hook, and draw it through two loops on the hook three times. When working the first row of treble crochet on a foundation chain, start your first stitch in the fourth chain from the hook and always chain 3 to turn when the first stitch on the next row is to be a treble crochet.

Double Treble Crochet

Work as the treble crochet except wrap the yarn three times over the hook instead of twice and take two loops off four times instead of three.

153

Triple Treble Crochet
Work as the treble crochet except wrap the yarn four times over the hook instead of twice and take two loops off five times instead of three times.

Increasing and Decreasing
When it is necessary to increase in a single crochet stitch, the basic formula is to work 2 stitches in the same stitch, thus forming an extra stitch. The new stitch would also be worked in single crochet, since a new stitch is always worked in the same type of stitch as the original in which the increase is being made. In double crochet, for example, the stitch to be increased would be worked in double crochet, and in treble crochet it would be a treble crochet. To decrease in single crochet, work off 2 stitches as one, thus decreasing, or "losing," a stitch. Do this by drawing up a loop in the next single crochet, then draw up another loop in the following single crochet, wrap the yarn over the hook and draw it through all three loops at once. Again, since the same stitch pattern is always maintained, as in increasing, to decrease a double crochet stitch, work your first double crochet to the point where two loops remain on the hook, then yarn over and insert the hook in the next stitch, yarn over and draw through the stitch, yarn over and draw through two loops, yarn over and draw through the remaining three loops.

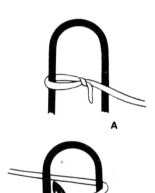

Hairpin Lace

Figure A
Tie a slipknot equal to half the adjusted width of the loom, remove the holding bar at the bottom of the loom, and place the left prong into the loop. Replace the bar.

Figure B
Wind the yarn around the right prong of the loom and across the back of it; then insert a crochet hook between the two strands of the loop to the left of the center of the loom, placing the hook under the front strand.

Figure C
Place the yarn that lies across the back of the loom over the hook and draw it through the loop, reach again for the yarn, place it over the hook, and draw it through the loop on the hook.

Figure D
Remove the hook from the stitch and reinsert it into the same stitch from the back. Turn the loom toward you now, from right to left, thus making a new loop of yarn around the back of the loom.

Figure E
Insert the hook between the two strands of the loop to the left of the center, placing it under the front strand. Then place the yarn that is across the back of the loom over the hook, draw it through, reach again for the yarn, and draw it through both loops on the hook, thus making a single crochet stitch, a series of which forms the "spine" of the work.

Repeat steps D and E for the desired length. If the loom becomes filled, remove the bar, slide all but the last four loops off the loom, replace the bar, and continue working as before for the desired length.

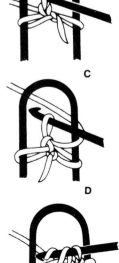

154

Knitting

Casting On

For your first stitch, make a slip loop on the needle, allowing a two-yard end of yarn for every 100 stitches that are to be cast on, more if the yarn is a heavier-than-average weight and less if it is lighter. Holding the needle in your right hand with the short end of the yarn toward you, *make a loop on your left thumb with the short end (A). Insert the needle from front to back through this loop (B), then place the yarn attached to the ball under and around the needle (C), draw the yarn through the loop, and pull the short end down to tighten it (D). Repeat from * for the desired number of stitches.

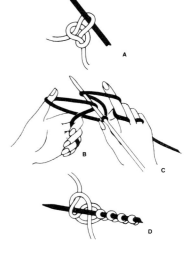

Knitting

Holding the needle with the cast-on stitches in your left hand with the yarn to the back of the work, *insert the needle in your right from the left to right through the front of the first stitch, wrap the yarn completely around the right needle to form a loop, slip the needle and loop through the stitch, and then slip the stitch just worked off the left needle. Repeat from * across all the stitches on the left needle.

Purling

*Holding the yarn in front of the work, insert the right needle from right to left through the front of the first stitch on the left needle, wrap the yarn completely around the right needle to form a loop, and slip the stitch just worked off the left needle. Repeat from * across all the stitches on the left needle.

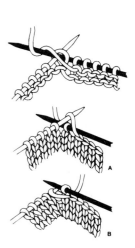

Binding Off

Knit the first 2 stitches, *insert the point of the left needle into the first stitch on the right needle (A), lift this stitch over the second stitch, and then drop it off the needle (B). Repeat from * across the necessary number of stitches to be bound off. When all the stitches are to be bound off at the end of a piece of work and just one stitch remains, break off the yarn and draw the remaining strand through the stitch. All binding off should be done very loosely so that there is a sufficient amount of elasticity to the finished edge.

Increasing

Insert the right needle from right to left through the back of the next stitch on the left needle, then wrap the yarn completely around the needle to form a loop (A), slip the needle and loop through to the front (thus forming a new stitch on the right needle), and then knit the same stitch on the left needle in the usual manner (B). Slip the stitch off the left needle.

Decreasing

Insert the right needle through 2 stitches on the left needle and work these 2 stitches together as one.

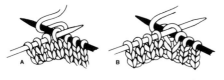

Picking up Stitches

Picking up stitches—often necessary around a neck or an armhole—is always done on the right side of the work and is usually started at a seam edge, such as the top of one shoulder for neck stitches or at the underarm for an armhole shaping. Stitches are picked up by inserting the right needle through the center of the desired stitch, placing the yarn around the needle, and drawing the yarn and the needle through the stitch, thus forming a new stitch on the right needle. The number of stitches to be picked up on any given piece of work should be distributed evenly so that the work lies flat.

Stockinette Stitch

Perhaps the most basic stitch used in knitting, the stockinette stitch is worked by alternating one row of knit stitches on the right side of the work with one row of purl stitches on the wrong side.

Macramé

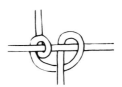

Horizontal Double Half Hitch

Tie each cord twice around the foundation, as shown.

Square Knot Button

Tie three square knots, pull filler cords up through top (see diagram) back down, and tie one square knot directly beneath button to complete.

Lark's Head

Draw ends of cord through center loop.

Half Square Knot

Tie, in three steps as illustrated, the first half of the square knot.

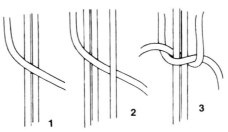

First Half of Knot

Square Knot

Tie the half square knot followed by the three steps for the second half of the knot below.

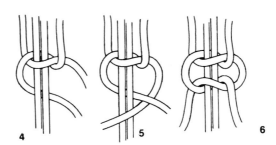

Second Half of Knot

Slipknot

The simplest knot in all needlework, tie this one as shown.

Latchet Hooking

Figure A

Fold a piece of yarn in half over the shank of your hook just below the latch.

Figure B

Holding the two ends of yarn between the thumb and index finger of your left hand and holding the latch down with the index finger of your right hand, insert the hook under the double horizontal threads of the canvas and then bring it up through the space directly above them, having the latch of the hook in position now above the horizontal threads. Draw the hook slightly toward you until the latch is at a right angle to the shank.

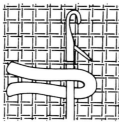

Figure B

Figure C

Bring the ends of the yarn over the shank of the hook, which is now positioned between the latch and the hooked end.

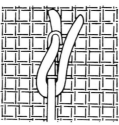

Figure C

Figure D

Pull the hook through the canvas, drawing the ends of the yarn through the loop.

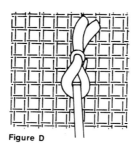

Figure D

Figure E

Pull the loose ends to tighten the knot.

Figure E

157

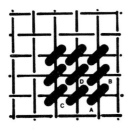

Needlepoint and Embroidery

Continental Stitch

Beginning at the right edge of the canvas, bring the thread up through point (A), down through point (B), up through point (C), down through point (D), and continue across the row in this way. For the second row, the canvas may be turned upside down and the row worked as the first, or the thread may be cut and the next row started again at the right edge.

Cross-Stitch

Bring the thread up through the canvas from the wrong to the right side at point (A) and then down from right to wrong side at point (B). Continue working across the canvas in this way for the desired number of stitches. Return across this same row to complete the second part of the crosses by bringing the thread up at point (C) and down at point (D).

French Knot

Bring thread through from wrong to right side of the fabric at point (A) and wrap it around the needle once or as many times as desired. Then pass the needle down through the fabric at point A. The completed stitch should look like Figure 3 below.

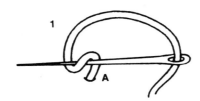

Kalem Stitch

Bring the thread up through the canvas from the right side at point (A) and then down from right to wrong side at point (B). Continue working vertically downward in this way for the desired number of stitches. Starting at the bottom of the next row, bring the thread up at point (C), and down at point (D) and continue in this manner.

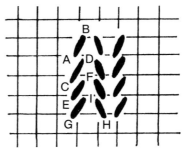

Lazy Daisy or Loop Stitch

Bring the thread through at the base of the petal on the traced line; then loop the thread around the needle and pass the needle back through the fabric, bringing it up at the center top of the petal with the thread under the needle. Make a small stitch over the loop to hold it in place, pass the needle through the fabric, and bring it up at the base of the next petal.

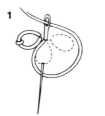

158

Outline Stitch

Bring the thread through at point (A) on a traced line and then pass the needle through the fabric from (B) to (C). Next, pass the needle through from (D) to (B). Continue working in this manner for the length desired.

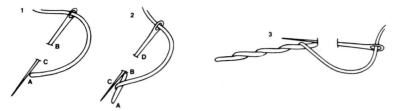

Overcast Stitch

Bring thread through two thicknesses of fabric in one motion, as shown.

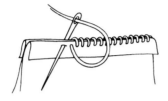

Running Chain Stitch

This stitch is worked along a traced or other established line. Bring the thread up through a given line at any point to be marked (A), pass the needle through from (A) to (B), and then pull it through. Continue in this manner, passing the needle through from (A) to (B), for the desired length.

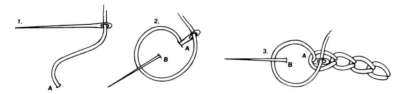

Satin Stitch

Bring the thread through at (A) along any traced or other established line. Then pass the needle down through the fabric at (B) on another established line at the opposite side of the stitch. Carry the needle across the back of the material and pass it through at the point next to (A). Continue to work in the same manner as for the first stitch.

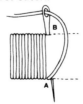

Straight Stitch

Bring thread through at (A) along a traced or other established line and pass the needle through the fabric at (B). Continue to work in this manner.